Stray Tales of the Big Bend

Number Forty-seven:
THE CENTENNIAL SERIES OF THE ASSOCIATION OF FORMER STUDENTS,
TEXAS A&M UNIVERSITY

Stray Tales OF THE *Big Bend*

By ELTON MILES
Photographs by Bill Wright

Texas A&M University Press
COLLEGE STATION

Library of Congress Cataloging-in-Publication Data

Miles, Elton, 1917–
    Stray tales of the Big Bend / by Elton Miles ; photographs by Bill
Wright. — 1st ed.
        p.   cm. — (The Centennial series of the Association of Former
Students, Texas A&M University ; no. 46)
    Includes bibliographical references and index.
    ISBN 0-89096-534-X (cloth). — ISBN 0-89096-542-0 (pbk.)
    1. Tales—Texas—Big Bend Region.   2. Legends—Texas—Big Bend
Region.   3. Big Bend Region (Texas)—History.   I. Title.
II. Series.
GR110.T5M536   1993
398.2'09764'93—dc20   92-39729
                                                  CIP

For
JAMES, WILLIAM, and MYRTLE

Contents

Preface

THE Big Bend country is a mysterious place. There the sound of jingling mystery bells in the night denote treasure, unkindled fires show just where to dig, ancient sacrificial dances bring rain and pieces of clay jigsaw puzzle hidden on a bluff tell of European presence around A.D. 300.

It is — or has been — a violent place. Tales report shoot-outs between badmen and the law, and history recounts the bloody raid on Glenn Springs during the Mexican Revolution and the robbery and kidnapping at Boquillas. The accounts here, together with what is told in the bandit, cowboy, and trooper chapters of *More Tales of the Big Bend,* should provide the most fully detailed account yet of Big Bend border raids between 1910 and 1918.

The Big Bend country is also a pious place. Some cowboys became preachers to bring their partners to Christ. Two of the most renowned camp meetings anywhere occur in this region each year, founded in early days by Big Bend ranch families and their cowhands.

The Big Bend is an uneven place. What has gone on and what goes on now in the Big Bend is uneven. Big Bend people, as individuals, are uneven. You can take one look at the Big Bend country and see that it is uneven. Dramatic variety abounds from the silent deserts and mountains.

This book could not have been put together without the ad-

10 *Preface*

Anne Ellis and Gilbert Sanchez, Odessa; Bernice and Jack Mc-
Gee, Fort Worth; Donald and Reva Uzzell, Brownsville and
Bastrop; Miriam Lowrance, Charles David, and Dr. Frank W.
Daugherty, Alpine; Barbara Maughmer, Terlingua; Russell Drake,
Lake Elsinore, California; Russell Gardenier and Dr. J. Charles
Kelley, Fort Davis; Fritz Kahl of Marfa and the Bloys Camp
Meeting Association; Meleta Bell in the Archives of the Big Bend
and Betty Dyess in the Department of Literature and Language,
Sul Ross State University; and especially, my lifelong partner,
Lillian Neale Miles.

PART I
Mysteries in the Desert

1.

Terlingua Desert Tales

UNDER A SKY that spreads from everywhere to yonder, the Chisos Mountains and Terlingua Desert seem quietly to contemplate a majestic secret they will never impart. Here is the setting of tales more elusive than regal.

The bells, for instance. Terlingua native and automechanic Earl Anderau had listened to yarns about the bells all his life but had never heard them. He said that several of his Mexican friends, making night camp at Adobe Walls with their freight wagons and mules, heard an unexplainable jingling of bells, or maybe harness chains. Neither that night nor the next morning could they find anything that could have made such a sound— only greasewood, sotol, and shin-stabbing dagger plants called *lechuguilla*.

Where the highway from Alpine to Big Bend National Park descends to the Terlingua Desert, it now bypasses the old dirt road that runs near the place called Adobe Walls. Now crumbling, the walls are the remains of an unfinished corral on the old G-4 Ranch, remembered mainly because of a shoot-out there in 1886. The shoot-out, however, has nothing to do with the bells. More about it later.

Early one August in the 1950s, Odessa schoolteacher Anne Ellis, her mother Lola, and some friends toured the Big Bend in two cars to see the sights and take a break from their classes at Sul Ross State University. Under a bright, full moon Anne, in the lead car, was talking to friend Shirley,

> when all of a sudden I was interrupted by the clear tinkling sound of many little bells, or of chains, in a definite rhythm loud and clear, audio perfect in volume. It was as if I was hearing, from out of the past, a strange ritualistic dance by Indians with bells on their arms and their legs, or as if harnessed horses with rattling chains were traveling fast. My hair stood on end, my heart skipped a beat, and not a word did I utter. I scarcely drew a breath, and Shirley seemed glued to the foot-feed of the car and the sound traveled with us.

As they traveled along in "shock and wonder," their friend Net awoke on the back seat and exclaimed, "What's that? What's that? What's that?" Listening hard to the bells, neither Anne nor Shirley answered. Then, Anne said, "the sound disappeared as it had come, suddenly."

Scanning the landscape for a clue, Anne saw "nothing except the greasewood, the moon, and the cold, impersonal faraway mountains."

The car with their companions caught up, and, when both had stopped, Anne asked, "Did you hear that back there?"

Dorothy, driver of the second car, said "I heard chains or something!" So had Lola.

Later, discussing the experience in their quarters at Alpine, Anne remarked, "It has been said that sound never dies, and if that is so, perhaps the bells were an echo of the past."

Some years later, Anne learned of a Hispanic explanation of the bells. Working for Anne in Odessa was a roofer called Manuel. He said that his grandfather was one of the mule drivers who had camped at Adobe Walls and had heard the jingling more than once.

The sound of bells, he said, is a sort of treasure signal, apparently not confined to Adobe Walls. They jingle in the night, he said, only for those who have been chosen to find a treasure, but the lucky hearer must first follow a ritual. They must remember the date on which they heard the bells and return on an anniversary to the spot where they heard them. Then, in the distance, they will see a fire on top of a mountain. The seeker must go toward the fire, but the fire will go out before they reach it. When they reach the spot where the fire was burning, they will find a mound of ashes. Now they must dig, for under those ashes lies the treasure.

In fact, Manuel said that he was himself one of the chosen. Alone one night in the mountains, he heard the tinkle of bells.

"*Qué pasa?*" he said to himself. ("What's going on?")

Then he remembered — treasure! He looked around the mountain tops, and there it was — a small fire twinkling high on a peak. Knowing the trail well, he set out walking toward the flame; he climbed and puffed as the trail grew steeper. He remembered that when the trail reached the top, it would perch him on a hogback knob that looked straight down dangerously high cliffs on all sides.

Then Manuel's discretion overcame his avarice. "Here I am," he thought, "all by myself. If I climb to the top and dig up the treasure, how do I know that on my way down the trail will not be blocked? What good is the treasure without my life? Who would know what happened to me?"

At this point Manuel's decision was easy to reach. He came down the mountain and went home, to let the sleeping riches lie.

I myself have heard mystery bells, not at Adobe Walls in the dark, but in broad daylight at the northeast corner of Alpine in the Ranchito residential development. In March of 1990 my wife, Lillian, and I were talking outside the unfinished house of another couple when I heard a ringing sound.

"Was that your telephone?" I asked.

"We don't have a phone yet," the neighbor replied. "It sounded like a tinkling."

I agreed that it did sound more like jingling little bells than a regular telephone. Neither Lillian nor our other friend heard it.

It looks as though Fate has elected me and that neighbor to

find the treasure. But, as it did not occur to me to record the date, I don't know when to get together with her again to hear the bells.

Now, about that shoot-out. On the Circle Dot Ranch southwest of Marathon, cowboy Jim Davenport lay down and went to sleep on his roundup job, only to let a good many cows get away and to be kicked awake and fired by the roundup boss, a man named Kincaid. Stirring up his own venom, Jim concluded that the range boss, "Old Man" Hereford, had reported him to Kincaid. Forthwith, he got drunk, hung two pistols on himself, called Hereford out of his shack, shot and killed him. On horseback he struck out for Mexico, passing through the G-4 spread, where his brother Jeff was punching cattle. The Rio Grande was "swimming" (flooding), his horse drowned, he lost one of his pistols, and he limped back to find a cow camp.

When Bass Outlaw and another Texas Ranger rode into the G-4 camp, they spread their bedrolls close to Jeff's. Some say they were actually looking for Jim, while others say they just happened along.

Sure enough, Jim hobbled into camp that night, tired and thirsty. Using the dipper, he drank from the bucket that hung under the arbor.

He called out, "Jeff!"

He was answered by two Texas Rangers, their pistols pointed at him. One said, "Put your hands up."

Jim did not obey. He started shooting, and from behind a wagon, the Rangers fired back. Thus rattled awake, cowboys scrambled like rabbits with the snapping jaws of a coyote at their tails. One was so mixed up that he hunkered down for cover against a wall on the wrong side, bullets kicking dirt out of the adobe all around him.

Jim, with two slugs in him, got away, walked a trail back to a spring, and hid out just over the next hill. Near sunup he saw the Rangers ride off, and in the G-4 camp he was welcomed as one of the bunch. The men dressed his wounds and sent him on his way with grub and a fresh horse.

In Mexico near San Carlos, south of Lajitas, he lodged with a Mexican woman, who nursed him back to health. Then along came an apparent elderly Mexican who asked to talk with this daring man. A reward of $500 had been offered to anybody who would bring Davenport in, and, in disguise, Texas Ranger Jim Miller was going to try. Luckily for Miller, Davenport told about the Adobe Walls shooting from his bed.

Still in Spanish, the Ranger asked, "May I see your gun?" Davenport pulled it from under his pillow and handed to his visitor.

Miller pointed Davenport's own six-shooter at him and said, now in English, "You're my prisoner. Get up from there and come on."

Miller conducted Jim Davenport back to Texas, collected the reward, and in effect sent him to the penitentiary. After getting out, Davenport disgraced himself somehow in Cotulla, Texas, and was shot dead by a policeman. That was in 1899.

The same year, Bass Outlaw took leave from Company D, near Alpine, to ride as an armed guard conducting burro trains of silver from a mine in Mexico up to the railroad at Marathon for shipment. Located at Sierra del Carmen, about eighty miles south of Boquillas, the Fronteriza Mine was operated by a kinsman of Ranger captain John B. Jones. Though the mine produced well, the owner, for fear of bandits, could not deliver the bullion to market. He asked Jones to lend him "three of the toughest men in Texas" to protect the little caravans, promising to pay them well. Calling for volunteers and attending to their discharge from the Texas Ranger force, Jones sent John R. Hughes, Walter Durbin, and Bass Outlaw.

Before the men left Company D, Jones reminded Hughes of how unruly Bass could be when he drank, which was often. "If he starts trouble down there," he warned, "you'll all face a firing squad." Apparently Bass promised to lay off the stuff while in Mexico.

On the day after their 160-mile horseback journey from Marathon to the Fronteriza, the three Texans headed back north with a half-dozen burros, each laden with bars of silver amounting to about 150 pounds and driven by Mexican handlers. Along the entire trail, they passed through only one village, Villa de Muchos, with less than fifty people.

In the jagged mountains and countless arroyos were plenty of places for bandits to hide for a sudden attack. As the group plodded along, the Mexican guards stayed with the burros while the three Texans deployed themselves otherwise. Durbin rode up the trail about fifty yards ahead, while Bass and Hughes popped through the brush at some distance on each side, ranging out sometimes a quarter of a mile. The eyes of all men were constantly scanning every inch of the rocky, thorny landscape. Several times, pistols ready, the outriders galloped back to the burros to confront approaching horsemen, who always turned out to be innocent travelers.

That first, tedious 320-mile round-trip took them about six weeks. With their increased knowledge of the country, each of the next two trips required only about a month. They had delivered, apparently, about two-thousand pounds of silver.

At the Fronteriza, in an adobe hut provided by the company, they took a few days of well-deserved rest, loafing around the mining camp. Up to this point, Bass Outlaw had gritted his teeth and had refreshed himself only with soda pop and water. Along about dark one evening, however, a frightening change was signaled by a pistol shot that startled Hughes and Durbin as they sat in their adobe, cleaning their guns. They ran to the mine commissary, looked through the door, and there was Bass, drunk as a hoot owl.

With a pistol in each hand, Bass had lined up a number of workmen against a wall, their hands up high. Weaving back and forth, he uttered grave threats. A Mexican lay dead on the floor with one of Bass's bullets in him. Flat against the wall out front, Hughes and Durbin watched for a chance to calm Bass down.

The errant Ranger staggered backward to the door, halted, and exclaimed, "The first man that comes out of here after me, gets this!" And he blasted off a shot through the floor.

When Bass stepped out of the store, Hughes and Durbin pinioned his arms and twisted his wrists until he dropped his pistols. The small, frenzied Bass fought the two tall, powerful men so furiously that they cracked him on the head with one of his own pistols. They picked him up, carried him to the adobe, and stretched him out on his bunk.

Quickly they armed themselves to the eyebrows and piled weapons and ammunition on the table, determined not to surrender Bass to a mob. Even if they were not overpowered now, the chance of all three making it across the desolation back to Marathon alive was mighty slim.

Soon, here the pursuers they came. In close order a number of Mexicans walked toward the hut. The Rangers blew out the lamp and braced themselves for the worst. Rifle across his arm, Hughes stepped out to parley. Durbin covered him from a window. The "mob" halted.

A mine foreman stepped forward to speak his piece. "Señor," he said, "we are not mad about this. That Pedro, he was a *malo*. He got what was coming to him. He deserved it."

Thus were the Rangers relieved of the dread of possible extinction. Hughes thanked the men for expressing their gratitude and was silently grateful that an international incident had been averted by Bass's fortuitously shooting the right man.

The sobered Bass was apologetic but said that Pedro had pulled a knife on him. He renewed his promise not to drink — that is, not until they were back in Texas.

Without incident, the guards led two more pack trains to Marathon, having now transported about four thousand pounds of silver in all. Upon returning from the latter of these treks, they found the mine shut down and padlocked. Clerks still in the office explained that the Mexican government had ordered that, for the time being, no more silver could be taken out of the country from the Fronteriza. They paid the silver guards in full, whereupon Bass Outlaw and his two companions rode back to Texas to reenlist in Company D at Alpine.

Treasure and violence also mark a sordid episode in the history of a family that has dwelled for more than a century in the Terlingua Desert country. While today many of the family have moved to the city and attained affluence, the legend of the unfortunate Jesusita is still told and was passed along by one of her granddaughters to Anne Ellis.

About 1870, Jesusita was a small Indian girl whose mother was given to vitriolic rages. On one occasion, when Jesusita was about twelve years old, her mother soared into a violent temper because of something she did or did not do and screamed, "I don't want you anymore!"

At this moment a stranger called "the Spaniard" rode by on a white horse. When the mother saw him, she shouted, "Do you want this girl? If you do, take her! I don't want her!"

The man considered Jesusita's puerile beauty and light complexion, then said, "Yes, I'll take her." The hapless child was mounted behind the saddle, and she rode away with her new master to his property at the foot of the Chisos, where he owned a trading post.

Jesusita's master was more abusive than her mother, if that is possible. He treated her like a slave and lashed her often with a whip. When she grew up, he married her, but was just as cruel as ever, refusing even to let her have any money of her own.

Sometimes, when he was away from the store on business, he left Jesusita in charge. In vain hope of accumulating a little something for herself, she would put back some of the money when she sold items to customers. Upon his return the Spaniard would demand the money she had taken in — all of it — every cent.

She refused. The two set to shoving, slapping, and screaming, but Jesusita could never hold out. She would fetch a bucket from its hiding place, scatter the money on the floor, and yell, "There is your old money! Take it! Take it!"

Smugly, the Spaniard would crawl about the floor, gather up the cash, count it, and then secure it. This confrontation became almost ceremonial, repeated many times over many years, and Jesusita always lost.

But finally the whip hand became hers when the Spaniard

went blind. In her husband's old age, she gave him back every lashing he had given her as a girl.

Furthermore, the sightless old man was deprived of his money. Times were poor and not much was coming in at the store, but he had cash hidden in the mountains. Over the years he had occasionally ridden off with his hoarded money to hide it. He would be gone all day and all night. Now, his eyesight gone, he could not possibly find his way to the cache, but he refused to tell anyone where it was buried, and Jesusita managed to prevent anybody's going with him as a guide. When he, and then Jesusita, died, his treasure still lay buried somewhere on a lower slope of the Chisos.

Then there came to one of their grandsons a possible clue that might lead its recovery. In several of his dreams, Jesusita appeared and showed him the exact mountain on top of which the money lay in the ground. The grandson, as the granddaughter told Anne Ellis, should climb this mountain, and when he reached the top, the shadow of grandfather "Spaniard" would appear and point to the precise spot where his descendant should dig. However, by 1968, when he told the story, the grandson had followed none of these instructions but had let the treasure, if any, stay put.

Another mystery of the Terlingua Desert is how the place got its name. There is no such word as Terlingua in the Spanish language; nor is there one for Los Chisos, the mountains, though a folk understanding once was that *chiso* meant ghost in Spanish. When this explanation was dispelled, another claimed that *chiso* was an Indian word for ghost. Digging into eighteenth-century Spanish documents of Mexico, however, made it clear that Los Chisos were so called because the Chisos branch of Apaches wintered there. An Apache linguist, Dr. Harry Hoijer, helped to establish the opinion that *chiso* is a Spanish version of *chishi*, the Apache's name for himself, meaning "forest dweller." But what about Terlingua? The origin and meaning of its name have been even more slippery than those of Los Chisos.

It is well known that the name of Terlingua was used early to designate an Indian-Mexican farming community on the lower end of Terlingua Creek nor far from where Santa Helena Canyon empties into the Rio Grande. Terlingua Desert rancher Walter Fulcher heard from old Mexicans in the 1920s and 1930s, that it had been an Indian camp before 1800. About 1850, scalphunter John Glanton wiped out that camp.

In the 1880s when the Marfa and Mariposa Mining Company dug out quicksilver near Lajitas, the old Terlingua's name was applied to its settlement of workers and their families. When that mine played out in the early 1900s, the people and the name moved to the present site, where the Chisos Mining Company flourished. Most of the Mexicans, called the new place Chisos and referred to the old settlement as Terlingua Abajo or Terlingua Vieja (Lower Terlingua or Old Terlingua).

The vexing puzzle remains: How did Terlingua get such a name and what, if anything, does it mean? In one of two strong oral traditions, Terlingua is said to be a corruption of *tres lenguas*, which means both "three languages" and "three tongues." It is said that the languages spoken in that region were "Indian," Spanish, and English. In 1941, amateur historian Henry T. Fletcher of Marfa wrote, "Tres Lenguas refers to a legend that Apaches, Comanches, and Shawnees formerly lived there in peace." Shawnees in any numbers, however, were immigrants who seem to have lived no farther west than the Brazos Reservation, northwest of Fort Griffin on the Clear Fork of the Brazos.

In the second oral tradition, "three tongues" denotes not languages but three watercourses. Some have said that Terlingua Creek joins two other unnamed streams to make up the three "tongues." But Fletcher noted that Terlingua Creek receives the waters of Goat, Calamity, and Crystal creeks. Presumably, they are the three "tongues," or branches, of the main stream.

By 1900, apparently, a completely different explanation had developed, soon to be smothered by the "three tongues" idea current not only orally but in print. In 1980 it was resurrected by

Dr. Ross Maxwell, geologist and the first superintendent of the Big Bend National Park.

In an informal conversation with students in his Terramar Adventure Club geology seminar at Terlingua Ranch, Dr. Maxwell relayed what Dr. Robert T. Hill had told him in the early 1930s. Then in his seventies, Dr. Hill was a geologist of world renown and a feature writer for the *Dallas Morning News*. In 1899, as head of the congressionally mandated Texas Geological Survey, he had led his party through the Big Bend canyons.

According to Dr. Hill, there was an Indian village near the mouth of Terlingua Creek, and "those Indians were noted for making a certain type of rug or blanket, which was highly prized by the cowboys throughout the region as saddle blankets." Such a blanket cost more than the store-bought variety but was considered a status symbol. "Every cowboy and vaquero," therefore, "who could scrape enough money together wanted one." The Indians' word for this blanket was "terlingua," and as result — said Dr. Hill to Dr. Maxwell to the seminar pupils, one of whom wrote about it — the village where they were made and the surrounding area were named Terlingua. Dr. Maxwell was reported as saying that this was "his favorite version of the explanation of the name."

As these conflicting versions and their variations cannot be reconciled, perhaps none is true.

Fulcher was told of documentary evidence that since the late 1600s, both Terlingua and Terlingua Creek have borne these names as a written Spanish version of an Indian word. In 1912, when Fulcher was herding goats near Sheffield, Texas, his eighty-year-old Mexican companion gave him this account:

As a young man, the man said, he studied for the priesthood in Mexico. Growing disenchanted with ecclestiastical life, he abandoned it. As he had heard much about Texas and had read about it in books and old church documents, he "northed" across the Rio Grande for good. Sul Ross student Paulina Peneda, citing a now lost Fulcher manuscript, said the man told Fulcher of "a very old document — he did not remember the date on it —

but it must have been two hundred years old or more." (If he studied for the priesthood at the age of twenty-five, the document could date to about 1657.) "It mentioned Terlingua Creek, and an Indian village of the same name, where the creek joined the Rio Grande. This man could not read the paper very well, since it was faded and the [archaic] Spanish was strange to him. But there was no doubt of the name the Indians called the village. It was 'Terlingua' just as it is today." The fact is, however, that the name of the creek has not always been so.

Evidence to back up an Indian origin of the name suggests that Terlingua is a Spanish form of an obsolete Apache borrowing from a Uto-Aztecan dialect. The word is *tezlingo*, said to designate an intoxicating plant and perhaps intoxicating drinks. In 1949, writing about her home town, Ms. Peneda said that in Terlingua she knew

> an old Mexican who could neither read nor write, but said that when he was a small boy his mother married a middle-aged man who had spent most of his life as a trader among wild Indians, and that his stepfather knew more about Indians than anybody he ever saw. His stepfather accounted for the word Terlingua in this way. He said there was a certain narcotic plant that grew only in the Terlingua area, that the Indians were fond of getting lit upon. He did not know what this plant was but said the Indians called it *tezlingo* and called the creek by the same name.

The plant — or plants — in question could be sotol, maguey, or peyote, or all three, from which alcoholic liquids have been derived since primitive times. Fermented heads of these plants, when eaten, induce intoxication. It is sotol which is the most abundant on the Terlingua Desert.

In Apache dialects — and in Big Bend Hispanic dialectics today — there are names for homemade intoxicants phonetically akin to *tezlingo*. Referring to Fulcher, Ms. Peneda said, "In his reading about the Apaches, he read that they made an intoxicant which they called *tezuino* or *tezwino*, which is also some kind of wild plant."

In Alpine in the 1940s and 1950s, the mother of Abelardo

Baeza (now a professor at Sul Ross) made a mildly alcoholic beverage she called *tezuino*. Though her version was a peach brandy, the old name fit the product. In 1988 Frances Tovar spoke of Alpine Hispanics making *tezuino* from corn, which she said was good. In his *Diccionario de Mexicanismos* (1974), Francisco J. Santamaria identified corn as the traditional ingredient of *tezguino*, the name of which he links with the Tarahumaras of the Chihuahua region. Many studies, past and present, of Apache groups speak of that people's ancestral ceremonial drink as *tezwin* or *tizwin* made from corn.

It is *tezlingo*, however, that documentary evidence in English supports as the probable source of the name Terlingua. These references allude only to the creek, not a settlement. These sources make it clear that Terlingua was not so pronounced or spelled before 1860 and that forms similar to the earlier *tezlingo* persisted into the twentieth century.

In their reports early explorers tried to spell the name as they understood it from oral pronunciations by local Mexicans and perhaps Indians. It seems certain that the earliest had no previous spelling to follow. Their ears untrained in phonetics, these observers could only approximate what they heard from the natives. In the English alphabet there is no symbol — nor in speech a sound — to approximate the Spanish rolled *r*, much less the often strange gurgling and clicking consonant sounds of Indian dialects. But the observers did their best.

In 1860 the creek was repeatedly called "Lates Lenguas" by U. S. Army explorer Lt. William S. Echols in his report. He examined the Terlingua Desert in 1859. In 1866 a map in *Johnson's Texas* called the stream Latislengua Creek, very near the spelling by Echols.

It is apparent that both Echols and Johnson joined the Spanish article *la* (the) to the creek's name, so the names reduce to "Tes Lengua and Tislingua, both of which approximate *tezlingo*. In Echols and Johnson lies the firmest evidence for judging *tezlingo* to be the source of Terlingua.

A later form of the ghost town's name — and a supposed

meaning—was given currency when C. A. Broadbent, having toured the Big Bend in 1883, referred to "Terlingua"—apparently the village—"on old maps Tres Lenguas, three languages, Indian, Spanish, and English." Apparently no other researcher has seen such a map, a fact that suggests Broadbent's source probably was oral.

In 1900 Brewster County property records refer to Tas Lingas Creek, and in the 1950s Brewster County Clerk Worth Frazier said that some old-timers still called the creek Tas Lengua (not much different from *tezlingo*).

By 1902 the spelling and pronunciation Terlingua had all but replaced other forms. In January of that year surveyor O. W. Williams of Fort Stockton wrote of "Terlingua Creek" and two months later told of "coming up the valley of Tasa Ling Creek." He datelined his letters "Terlingua," the village.

In 1941 Henry Fletcher observed that Terlingua Creek was variously called "Latis Lengua, Tres Lenguas, and Tasa Lingo, the latter probably an Apache name." The circle thus comes back near to *tezlingo* (Tasa Lingo).

It seems most likely that the place name Terlingua, as applied to both the creek and the village, is derived from *tezlingo*, which refers to some native plant such as sotol and the alcoholic drinks made from it. Sotol grows on the Terlingua Desert in great numbers.

Dr. T. N. Campbell, University of Texas anthropologist, has a special interest in Southwestern place names of American Indian origin. After looking over the hypothesis formed here, he expressed this opinion: "I am inclined to believe that Apache immigrants borrowed that word (*tezuino*) from some Uto-Aztecan-speaking group, and that somehow this was transformed into something close to Terlingua." In other words, *tezlingo* appears to be the source of both *tezuino* and Terlingua.

At least one mystery of the Terlingua Desert—the source and meaning of its name—may now be virtually dispelled.

2.

The San Vicente Rain Dance

"THERE is so much *Indian* in this!"

These words of an Italian priest in Presidio, Texas, described a locally devised ceremony performed periodically by people in his church. They also describe the San Vicente rain dance enacted farther down the Rio Grande in the Big Bend. Called *la matachina*, the colorfully costumed dance apparently was Aztecan in origin but European in its name and Christian modification. San Vicenteros believed that if they danced, it rained.

Basically, the San Vicente *matachina* is a fertility rite, acting out a story with three main characters. To climax hours of dancing, *el Viejo*, the evil old-man spirit of drought and sterility, tries to kidnap *la Malinche*, the young virgin, and is killed by the virile hero, *el Capitan*. The dancers then drink of *el Viejo*'s blood and smear themselves with it.

Such rites to ensure productivity in farm, flock, and family are as old as human effort to form a compact with the gods. Far newer is the concluding scene, in which *el Capitán* dedicates *la Malinche* to the service of Christ—a feature introduced at the urging of missionary *padres*.

The San Vicente version—or versions that developed as years went by—represents a blending of elements seen in the *matachina* performed in scattered Mexican and New Mexican villages. In these places, too, Christian themes were introduced to redefine the intent of the pagan ritual.

In 1895 *la matachina* came into the Big Bend with seventeen Mexican pioneer families who moved there with their wagons and animals from Comanche, Chihuahua. Settling across the Rio Grande from the hundred-year-old San Vicente, Mexico, they called their settlement by the same name, thereby creating another set of the many twin villages that straddle the border.

Congenial and hard-working, nearly all the people of the new San Vicente were kin to each other. Determined to survive on this sunbaked desert, each family — usually with three or four sons — staked out a piece of Texas state-owned land and cultivated their patch. They kept horses, burros, and a few goats and cows. Before long many of these families held deeds to their farmsteads and trusted in their *matachina* to pull them through. It seemed to work in Mexico — why not in the Big Bend?

At San Vicente, Texas, in about 1970, Crecencio Sanchez, age seventy-six, spoke of the organization, costumes, and movements in the ritual, but said little about the story and almost nothing about its Christian elements. As he told his interviewer, Gilbert Sanchez, in 1900 he was a six-year-old dancer in one of the four *matachina* "clans" that supplied four lines in the dance. He said, "The first tradition concerning *la matachina* is that it is held on May the third. We like to call it *el día de la Santa Cruz* [Holy Cross Day]. A group of people have the ceremonial dance at the foot of Santa Cruz Mountain." A map drawn by Gilbert shows this hill on the Texas side, while an earlier account places it in Mexico. Perhaps the river's course had changed.

A hierarchial organization governed the costuming of the dancers. Of the clans, Don Crecencio said: "They had ranks like today's army. The first ones in each line were the oldest of that group. These higher Indians wore armbands. The Indians next in line, called *saladolo razo*, wore a loincloth. The others were *saladodo*." It seems that the old man's terminology was a border dialect variation of *soldado* (soldier) and *soldado razo* (private soldier).

As reported by Frances Toor, Yaqui *matachines* in northwestern Mexico called themselves "soldiers of the Virgin." Forming a lay organization within the church, they were led by a chief with two assistants. The chief dancer, called *el Monarca*, also had two assistants. Membership was for life and included persons who vowed to join upon recovery from severe illness. Sometimes parents pledged their little boys when they were sick, and the youngsters would dance with the group when they were old enough — as may have been the case with little Crecencio Sanchez. Indeed, in earlier versions of the dance, *la Jovencita* (Malinche) had been played by a young boy dressed as a girl.

At San Vicente, the Don said, the *matachines* "painted their faces purple and red, with touches of white. Some painted a cross on their chin and a sign in the shape of a ponderosa tree on the right side of their face." One dancer, instead of painting his face, wore "an old man's mask with small holes for eyes and one hole for the mouth. His mask usually had lines for wrinkles." Here was *el Viejo*, the drouth-sterility demon.

In such dances elsewhere, *el Viejo* (or *el Abuelo* — grandfather) was a clown who wove in and out of the lines of dancers. As a clown, he seems to have had no importance other than to be amusing. Thus the padres seem to have altered the original function of the old, evil spirit.

For costumes, Don Crecencio said, "They wore pants and loin cloths. From this cloth they hung hollow sections of dried river cane and rattlesnake rattles in no particular design." A photograph of a later San Vicente ceremony shows as many as four fringe-like rows of hollow canes encircling a dancer's skirt, which seems to have replaced the loin cloth. Perhaps this dancer was *el Monarca*, as the skirts of two dancers behind him have only two rows.

Around his neck each man wore two strands of beads. For props, according to the don, "they would carry a board in the shape of a paddle in the left hand. On this *palma* [palm leaf] they would attach a mirror in the center, usually surrounded by broken pieces of mirror." The *palma* could represent three things: a weapon with which to slay evil, a sacrificial sword, or a phallus. In all three respects it represented the continuation of life.

"In the right hand," the don went on, "they carried a gourd. This gourd would be filled with pebbles and used as a rhythm instrument." The sound of the gourds was augmented by the rustling of the cane and snake-rattle fringes on the loin cloths. In this way each *matachine* was costumed from top to toe. On his head he wore a band of cane tubes "holding feathers that pointed in all directions," and on his feet, he wore Mexican moccasins.

When it was time to begin, the don recalled, "the dance started with the group divided into four lines, each headed by the oldest member." The number in a line depended on how many of its clan were present. The choreography was simple. "Staying in line, they would take two steps to the left and then one step to the right. At the same time, their bodies would go down on the left and up on the right. They would take one step back and two forward and then turn around in their places. They would make animal sounds while they danced." Frances Toor has written that at Tuxpan, Mexico, dancers in a venerable Aztecan ritual "emit in their masks hoarse cries, which sound like those made by mysterious animals."

After hours of going through their motions, the San Vicente *matachines* "would break up into two lines," said Don Crecencio. The purpose of the rite was achieved when "the four leaders would have a mock fight against the designated *Viejo*. He would be killed, and the others would dance by and cover him with their *palmas*." Concluding his account, the don said, "This would be the signal for the rain to begin, and, nine times out of ten, it would."

In 1910 J. O. Langford, owner of the Hot Springs health resort, put his wife Bessie and their two small daughters on horses and led them on foot along the five-mile river trail to San Vicente, Texas. They came to see the rain dance performed on Holy Cross Day at the end of a two-week period of communal prayer. The dance differed in many ways from that described by Don Crecencio.

During that fourteen-day period, families in every adobe, *jacal*, and dugout had prayed daily for rain. No man was allowed to touch alcohol through that time. Day after day people followed the village *jefe* (there was no priest) from field to field, where they knelt, prayed, and crossed themselves. Ahead of the people walked the *jefe* and two men bearing a *nicho*, a box with two poles for hand-carrying. In each field, as Haldeen Braddy described an even later performance of the ritual, the two carriers set the *nicho* on the ground, knelt with their faces in the dust, and "by various sounds and gesticulations, prayed to their various saints."

The *nicho* featured pictures of the Virgin Mary and Jesus and was decorated with pink paper roses and Christmas tinsel. The gathering of adornments for costumes and the *nicho*, as Langford told Ethel Nail, had been going on for months. The San Vicenteros collected tobacco cans (which were flattened and cut into pieces), paper flowers, ribbon, lace, embroidery, and small mirrors from boxes of popcorn or candy.

When the Langfords arrived, they were escorted across the river to where the people were kneeling to pray for the last field. They were startled as the *jefe* punctuated "amen" by blasting off six pistol shots into the air. Then all rose from their knees. Apparently the head of each farmstead provided the *jefe* with ammunition to frighten evil forces away by the noise. Or, as Ethel Nail said, to "cut the sky" and make way for rain.

The villagers then followed the *nicho* as the bearers took it to a small hill, *la loma de la Santa Cruz*. The *jefe* stood aside as the bearers struggled up the steep slope and, kneeling, set the box at the foot of a large, wooden cross. When the *jefe* fired his pistol again, the people crawled up the hill on hands and knees, with the *jefe* shooting in the air at regular intervals.

After more prayer, their voices rising and falling together, the crowd stood and, without a word, followed the *nicho* and the *jefe* back down the hill and across the fields to a tree. The bearers fixed the *nicho* in forks of the tree, where it would stay until it rained — except during the rain dance in the village. After it rained, it would be brought to the *jefe*'s house for safekeeping until it was needed again.

In the afternoon the *nicho* was taken down and placed under an arbor in front of the *jefe*'s adobe hut. "All of the Mexicans participated in the dance," said Langford, "but only the principal actors were in costume." These included *el Monarca*, the head man; *el Capitán* and *la Capitána*, the man and the woman; *la Malinche*, the young girl; and, of course, *el Viejo*.

Except for *el Viejo*, all wore red costumes. On their heads sat conical *monteras* decorated with small mirrors, pieces of shiny metal, turkey feathers, red rope fiber and horsehair, and small shells. Dangling from each long tunic was a six-inch fringe, each strand of which passed first through a four-inch cane then through a hole in a fragment of bright tin. In the dance these jangled against each other. Every dancer carried a gourd rattle and, instead of a *palma*, a bow and arrow splotched with red stain and red scraps of tin representing blood. (Prince Albert tobacco cans were red and may have provided the colored tin.) As described by Braddy and by Langford to Ethel Nail, the bows were two to three feet long and designed to serve as noisemakers. Each arrow passed through a hole in the center of the bow, where it was caught by a knob or a washer near the notched, feathered end of the shaft, making a loud twang. Each dancer carried a "blood-stained" *guapo*, or rattle.

The evil *Viejo* was distinguished by a hideous, wrinkled mask and tall mule ears. Dragging the ground from this headgear was a long, gray queue. Besides his *guapo*, he carried a snaky rawhide whip, which he cracked above his head as he pranced.

The afternoon rite began as *el Capitan* and *la Capitana* danced up under the arbor to the *nicho*, where *la Capitána* snapped her bow four times. When she shifted aside, all the others, two by two, repeated the same movements.

"Gradually," said Langford, "a circle was formed and the dance began, a prancy step accompanied by the measured rattling of gourds." Thus, in format this rain dance was different from that of earlier years as described by Don Crecencio. Langford said nothing of dancers' facing each other, crossing, and turning, nor did he use the term *matachina*. Also describing a circle of dancers, Braddy observed that the steps were "uniformly short" and the dance was "a kind of one-two, one-two-three step — hops up and down — varied only by side swings from the hips."

During these undulations, *el Monarca* punctuated the rhythm with loud whoops, and *el Viejo* split the air with whip cracks. "Dust rose," said Langford, "from scores of moccasined feet. . . . It was a weird sight and a fascinating one. It held us gripped there so that we lost all sense of time and were conscious only of sight, sound, and movement."

Periodically *la Capitána* signaled for the dancers to take a break. Some sitting on benches under the arbor, others standing or sitting on the dirt plaza, they talked, laughed, and smoked cigarettes until *la Capitána* ordered the dance to resume.

During the final hubbub of shuffling, rattling, jangling, whooping, and whip-cracking, *el Viejo* left the ring. Returning on a burro, he broke into the ring, grabbed the virgin *Malinche*, and tried to carry away the neighborhood's symbol of fertility. With his fiercest yell, *el Monarca* raised his bow and "shot" the evil spirit of impotence. *El Viejo* fell to the ground, and four times the others danced by his "corpse," first to "drink his blood" and pretend to smear it on their costumes and bows and arrows. On the second go-round, they laid their bows on his body; on the third, the arrows; and on the fourth, their *guapos*.

The rain dance over, the bearers removed the *nicho* from its place under the *jefe*'s arbor, carried it away, and set it up again in the tree. The earth was parched by a hot, windy April, and what few crops had been planted were scrawny and drooping. The level of the Rio Grande was below that of the irrigation ditches. That night stars gleamed in a clear sky. "By daylight," said Langford, "rain was pouring down and it continued to pour. By noon every *arroyo* was alive with water, and the Rio Grande had risen four feet." The fields were soaked. "Eagerly," said Langford, "the people planted their corn, pumpkin seed, and grain. Ten days later, the planting over, the rains fell again for four successive days. The river rose ten feet. A bountiful harvest was assured."

By the 1930s, to judge by Braddy's report, further changes marked the San Vicente rain dance. Musical instruments were introduced — fiddle, guitar, tambourine, and, in the climactic movements, a drum, as Langford also told Ethel Nail. As the dance began, not only *la Capitána*, but also the young girl — now called *la Jovencita* — carried a bow and arrow.

A rather significant change was the renaming of legendary Malinche with more common term, *la Jovencita*. Just why this change came about is unclear, but perhaps it was to purify her character. Into the 1970s in all the *matachinas* still performed in New Mexico pueblos, she still was called *la Malinche*, thought to signify goodness and bridal virginity. But historically, Malinche was the mistress and skilled interpreter of Hernán Cortez, of invaluable service to him in his conquest of Mexico. Though legend has it that she was Aztecan, she was in fact a Caribbean island native called Marina (woman of the sea). Because she was allied with their enemy, Aztecs gave her the derogatory name "Malinche," and even today on the Big Bend border, to refer to a woman as Malinche is an insult, suggesting "prostitute."

Nevertheless, Malinche became a revered figure among Mexican Indians, and her name seemed to lose its derogatory edge. She was a Mother Eve figure, as tradition holds that she bore the first *mestizos*, the children of Cortez. In this capacity she serves as a fertility figure. She also was said to have been the first Indian to teach Christianity to other Indians, giving her religious status. There is traditional ground, then, for *la Malinche* (or *la Jovencita*) to be presented before the holy *nicho* at the end of the rain dance. She strengthens the Christian element imposed on the originally pagan rain dance.

In the performance Braddy witnessed, when *el Viejo* tried to abduct *la Jovencita*, the dancers moved in a circle around him to "discomfit him with raucous noise of rattling gourds." After *el Capitan* "killed" *el Viejo*, the dancers threw their gourds on his body. Then, said Braddy, the dancers jogged single-file into the ring, symbolically smeared their reclaimed implements with the old man's blood, and resumed their places in the circle. At this point, a pounding drum joined the music and rhythm as the dancers triumphantly led *la Jovencita* to the *nicho* under the arbor.

Then began a nightlong fiesta with merrymaking and feasting to compensate for two weeks of prayer in the desert fields under a fireball sun. Braddy observed that the merriment was "also of a carnal kind," consistent with fertility rites as ancient as Dionysian orgy. He said also that *la Jovencita* "is altogether probably Our Lady and the Life Force."

Braddy said that "soon after" the rite was performed on the afternoon of June 16, it poured down rain, and then the planting began.

With population movement and urbanization in West Texas, something like the San Vicente *matachina* found itself in the barrio in Midland, Texas, in the 1920s. Head of the *Matachina* Clan there was Miguel Hernandez. Inez Sanchez described it for his son, Gilbert, who said, "My father's account of the dance was in many ways similar to that of Crecencio Sanchez." In a nonagricultural community, however, the need for rain was seldom urgent, and the ritual was put to other uses, as it had been elsewhere. "Often," said Gilbert, "the ceremony was performed by persons who vowed to celebrate the dance annually after they survived a serious illness or avoided a great tragedy. The vow enabled outsiders to become permanent members of the *Matachina* Clan for religious purposes." As an afterthought, Inez added, "This dance was also performed on May the third for the purpose of getting rain."

"At first," said Inez, "the dance remained the same [as that in San Vicente] except that the fiddle was introduced in the mu-

A   B

Midland rain-dance tune, as wordlessly chanted and beat out on a small drum. It was recorded on audio-tape by Mrs. Sanchez in Midland, Texas, in the 1950s. To avoid the use of ledger lines, the melody is notated one octave higher than performed.

It was chanted with eight repetitions. In the fourth, fifth, seventh, and eighth repetitions the melodic figure A was chanted at the key of A. At the end of the eighth repetition the notes at B were omitted. The notes above the staff denote the drum beats. The notation of "112" indicates the number of beats per minute.—Notation by Dr. Rex Wilson; drawing by Charles David.

sic." Photographs made in 1920 suggest that the allegory still was acted out—the rescue of *la malinche* from *el Viejo* by *el Capitán*.

Basically, costumes in Midland resembled those at San Vicente. Dancers would paint their face white with red on their lips and three red stripes on each side of the face. Some had pierced ear lobes, while others clipped on diamond-shaped mirror earrings with bands of gold or silver. Around their necks were strands of silver and gold beads. Headdresses consisted of multicolored feathers held by cloth bands decorated with triangular mirrors. Such mirrors also decorated streamers hanging down the back.

On their backs, said Inez, "They would wear a larger replica of the same design," and "their shirt sleeves would have more mirrors arranged in a straight line." A similar design "was repeated on the bell-shaped cuffs." Usually the dancers wore white shirts, and their trousers were "blue and made in a baggy style, held at the waist by a red band" and extending to just below the knee. Long white stockings completed the costume.

As they had in the older San Vicente ritual, the dancers carried decorated *palmas*, not bows and arrows. Gourds often were replaced by tin cans with pebbles inside and a stick handle decorated with crepe-paper streamers.

Gilbert noted that "the large number of women and children" taking part in his father's day was evidence "that the dance was dying out because of the reluctance of the adult male population to participate." The *matachina* was performed in Midland into the 1950s before it faded away completely.

The word *matachina* is not of American Indian origin. Brought to Mexico in the sixteenth century, it could derive from two sources. One theory is that it comes from the Arabic *mudawajjhin*, which means both "those who face each other" and "those who put on a face." Another is that the name means literally "Kill the Chinaman"— *Mata Chino* — or, in a broader sense, "Kill the pagan." The latter meaning probably would have been acceptable to the padres, who did their best to guide their Indian parishoners into Christianized versions of their ancient rites. To the dancers, of course, the word meant nothing except as a name for the dance and for themselves. Many forms of the *matachina* developed in Europe, including the English Morris Dance, and there were similarly many variations in Mexico and the Southwest borderlands.

As performed at San Vicente and elsewhere, however, the dance seems to have owed something to the Aztecs. In 1519 at Tenochtitlan (Mexico City), Bernal Díaz observed that some of Montezuma's entertainers "danced like those in Italy called the Matachines." With this brief remark, Díaz compared the Aztec dancers with clownish dancers of Europe, who have been described as masked men "ridiculously disguised" and striking each other with bladders or wooden swords. While clowning is part of many a Southwest borderlands *matachina*, no clowning as such has been reported as part of either the San Vicente or Midland versions. They seem to have been closer to an ancient Aztec ceremony.

The San Vicente rite differed from other versions also in that instead of a bull, *el Viejo* is killed. An 1881 version at Trinidad, New Mexico, featured, besides about sixteen male dancers, a resplendent *Monarca* (Montezuma), Malinche (his virgin girlbride in white), *el Viejo* (her father), *la Vieja* (her mother), Carrelampio (a boy, her brother) and *el Toro* (the bull). *El Viejo* (cracking his whip) and Carrelampio were clowns, while *la Vieja* was a mildly comic character. The business of *el Toro*, wearing a bull hide, was to prance about and disrupt the dancing however he could. Sometimes *el Viejo* tried vainly to control the bull. In turn, *la Malinche* begged each dancer to kill the bull, only to be refused. When she asked her father, *el Viejo*, he ceremoniously cocked a toy pistol and "shot" *el Toro*. Then *la Malinche* pantomimed catching the bull's blood in a large handkerchief and offering it to the onlookers, saying:

> *Tengan, tengan sangre*
> *Del toro quo mato mi padre.*
>
> (Take, take of the blood
> from the bull my father has killed.)

In several New Mexico *matachinas* of the 1940s and 1950s, which choreographer Flavia Waters Champe observed and studied, *el Toro* was thrown, tied, killed, and quartered by several *Viejos* (called *Abuelos*, grandfathers). Though the *matachinas* danced around the "dead bull," Champe reported nothing of blood. Rather, the dancers formed a cross through which principal characters wove in and out. Then came the finale of joyous thanksgiving and the exit, as the dancers went back into the building from which they had come.

It seems that the San Vicente/Midland rain dance — used also for other purposes — kept more pagan elements than those reported in New Mexico, in spite of the three-hundred-year effort of Catholic padres to Christianize it. In New Mexico versions, both *el Viejo* and *el Toro* were denigrated to the level of clown, while at San Vicente *el Viejo* was unmistakably an embodiment of evil and sterility. Furthermore, snapshots of the 1920 Midland dancers clearly show *el Monarca* (possibly serving as *el Capitán*), *la Capitána, la Jovencita* (Malinche), and *el Viejo*. While Flavia Champe saw the New Mexico dances as celebrating the spread of Christianity among the Indians by Malinche, the San Vicente version was much closer to a fertility rite. In the Big Bend, apparently, the padres had settled for about four nonpagan elements: (1) prayer in the fields before the dance began; (2) the dancers' offering their performance to Christ and the Virgin, as represented in the *nicho;* (3) the dedication of Malinche to the service of Christ; and (4) placing the *nicho* in a tree as a Christianized charm to invite rain. These dilutions were meant to suggest that God, not profane spirits, is in charge of the weather.

In New Mexico in the 1940s, dancers seemed to have no idea that their ritual had any meaning whatsoever — historical, religious, or magic. "We only know," said one, "when you dance it, it makes you feel good." Not so at San Vicente. They prayed, fired pistols, and danced to make it rain.

PART II
Over the Desert — and to the Orient

3.

The Orient Railroad

AS ALWAYS, Alpine citizens gazed across the pasture land, expecting an omen of prosperity to show itself to the Big Bend country. Milling about at the Kansas City, Mexico and Orient depot (later, the Santa Fe), they stared northward up the iron rails across the tan grass on November 2, 1930.

"Here she comes!"

The black dot on the horizon grew into a steam-snorting locomotive, and in rolled the hooting, clanging special train full of officials on the Orient's first trip from the United States all the way to Chihuahua City. The last segment of Orient track in the United States had been laid from Alpine to Presidio, completing the 647-mile line from Wichita, Kansas, through western Oklahoma and Texas. The planned stretch from Wichita to Kansas City was never built.

"Time will come," wrote editor J. M. Pouncey of the *Alpine Industrial News,* "when solid Pullman trains will stop at Alpine en route to the West Coast of Mexico."

A local cowman remarked, "That may be true, but they will be sidedoor Pullmans stoppin' at the loadin' pens."

J. Roy Spence told V. J. Smith of riding a mixed Orient train. It bore him out of Fort Stockton at 6:30 P.M. and deposited him in Alpine at 3:30 A.M., having averaged about six miles per hour. To rush the trip along, he helped prod cattle into the cars at the half-way stop of Hovey. On another occasion when a locomotive headlight blacked out at Hovey, train and passengers lingered until dawn before puffing on to Alpine.

They say that Good Samaritan train crews caused some tardiness in Orient service, so a poor roadbed and dilapidated equipment can't take all the blame. Lillian Miles was told that Orient workers would stop their train, walk over to the road, and help a motorist fix a flat. It is a fact that in Alpine the conductor held up the train's departure for Mrs. V. J. Smith while a friend drove back to her house to fetch the sack lunch she'd forgotten. The public is said to have returned the favors. Once a group of hunters at the Pecos River bridge near Fort Stockton flagged the train and had the crew down for a campfire dinner.

The time had seemed always at hand for the great idea of Arthur E. Stilwell, but it had a been a long time coming. The Orient Railroad was to cut four hundred miles of hauling from Kansas City to a Pacific port by heading south to Presidio, Texas, and Chihuahua City. Then it would wind over the Sierra Madre in Mexico to Topolobampo on the Gulf of California. There the natural harbor is eleven miles long and 270 feet deep and is said to be capable of hiding two United States fleets with plenty of room to spare. Since, compared with California routes, the new road greatly reduced both distance and freight charges from either eastern or midwestern railpoints to Mexico and South America, it would stimulate Asian commerce.

Early promotional literature made these claims and many others. The KCM&O would bring cattle from Texas to the feedlots of the Northwest. "San Angelo, the greatest wool market in the world, is on the line of this road." In the mountains of Mexico, eight to ten thousand feet of pine per acre could be cut and freighted to the treeless Southwest for building. The Fuerte River Valley, they said, grew an abundance of coffee, cotton, tobacco, oranges, and vegetables that only needed a rail outlet to the United States. "A new rival to the Alaskan and African gold fields is reported to have been discovered in Mexico." And "the key to this enterprise" was Port Stilwell, Topolobampo renamed, the golden gate to an immense Asian commerce. The KCM&O would

bring a real estate boom to every point on the route, the fold-
ers said.

But troubles lay ahead. What could not have been foreseen
were the irrigation of California and Arizona, the intense rivalry
of other railroads, protectionism, and revolution in Mexico, all
of which crippled the noble gesture to improve the domestic economy and international goodwill. The KCM&O was to become
a railroad with little purpose.

"The trouble with the Orient," said a cowboy, "is that it
don't start nowhere, it don't go nowhere, and there ain't nothin'
in between."

But you could not tell that to Arthur E. Stilwell, humani-
tarian tycoon of the Gilded Age, tireless money-raising builder,
and self-styled psychic. He was said to have been inspired by the
spirit world to build the Orient Railroad. He believed in the true
Gospel of Wealth — that a person should make money honestly
and do good with it, as well as enjoy it.

Born of a prosperous family in Rochester, New York, Stilwell left home at eighteen and started building a fortune. He
decided at the age of twenty-seven to go west and build railroads. At age thirty-two in 1889, he was president and builder
of the Kansas City Southern — destination, the then nonexistent
Port Arthur, Texas. He was inspired by the plight of midwestern
farmers who were burning their fifteen-cent corn for fuel. "The
misery of the West," he said, "was due to unjust prices the farmer
had to pay for the transportation of grain for export. I would
build a railroad to a southern port as an outlet for export shipment, reduce the cost of transportation by at least one-third, and
help redeem this great stretch of territory that was staggering
under the burden of corporate greed."

Idealistic and money-wise, Stilwell added, "The magnitude
of the resolution did not appall me. Let me say I simply had a
hunch." Some said he had visions, and he said that in his mind
he saw the girl he was going to marry. He met such a girl — her
name was Jenny Wood — and did just that.

The railroad hunch was as successful as the marital one. In

Stilwell's deciding where to terminate the railroad, inner voices warned him against Galveston, assuring him that city was doomed. When American financing proved impossible during the 1893 economic slump, spirits advised that he seek funds in the Netherlands; there he got all he needed to finish the road. By 1899 he had financed and finished construction of the KCS, along with the digging of the Port Arthur ship channel and harbor and letting in the Gulf waters. He acquired land, sold lots, and donated sites for the city of Port Arthur. In 1900, as prophesied, Galveston was devastated by the great hurricane.

More than six feet tall, his weight topping two hundred pounds, Stilwell displayed an exuberant personality. He was a model of sartorial perfection as he stepped from his glossy carriage to enter any of the several buildings he erected in Kansas City. He wore a brushy, upturned mustache, but shaved off his muttonchops after he read George Ade's quip, "If a man is cross-eyed it is a great disappointment; if a man is humpbacked it is an act of God; but if a man wears side whiskers it is his own fault."

A devout Christian, he composed hymns, which he played along with the standards on a pipe organ at home and on another in his private railroad car. This car was reputedly the most elegantly outfitted and betassled in the country. In it he entertained other businessmen, often of great wealth, and their families. The festivity sometimes consisted of hymn singing, with Stilwell at the keyboard.

Good luck came to Stilwell because of his handsomeness, imaginative grasp of details, and vivacious confidence. In his sickly childhood, he had finished only the fourth grade. He was, however, a mathematical wizard and, he said, "a word hound." In his lifetime he wrote several books and magazine articles. The talk about his spirit voices caused many to brand him as eccentric and not a few to call him insane. As often as good luck brought him prosperity, bad luck set him back.

In 1899, his year of triumph, ill fortune appeared in the form of John W. "Bet-a-Million" Gates, one of the Kansas City Southern investors. In a battle between midwestern and eastern tycoons for control, Stilwell rejected Gates's proposal that KCS properties be placed in receivership. Gates sought revenge, and eastern interests won when Gates, aided by W. H. Harriman, forced the railroad into receivership and Stilwell out of its presidency. They charged that Stilwell's company did not have sufficient funds to pay a forty-dollar printing bill, and a judge upheld them.

This misfortune ousted Stilwell just before the Spindletop oil discovery of 1901 that enriched both Port Arthur and the KCS. Later Stilwell wrote a vituperative book he called *Cannibals of Finance.*

Soon after his ouster from the KCS, on New Year's Day of 1900, friends gave Stilwell a consolation dinner. In his speech, having acknowledged defeat, he astonished all present with the announcement, "I have designed a railroad 1,600 miles long, which will bring the Pacific Ocean four-hundred miles nearer to Kansas City than any other. It will be 1,600 miles nearer to Central and South America than San Francisco and open the Orient to American business." In February he was off by train through El Paso and Chihuahua to Mexico City. The cooperation of Mexico was essential to his plan.

First, Stilwell made an important connection with Gen. Enrique Creel in Chihuahua. A major business leader, Creel already had planned the Chihuahua al Pacifico Railway. Early in 1900 it was completed from Chihuahua City to Minaca and aimed at Topolobampo. The general believed, "If all Mexico was a desert, it would pay to build the railroad for the Pacific business. If there was a wall at the Pacific, it would pay to build it for the great local business." He granted trackage rights to Stilwell along with his own right-of-way concessions and promptly was made vice-president of the Kansas City, Mexico and Orient Railroad.

At their Mexico City hotel, Arthur and Jenny Stilwell were

paid a social visit by a family member of Pres. Porfirio Díaz. The governors of Texas and several other states had telegraphed, urging the president to welcome his caller. Enemies also had wired Díaz, warning him to beware of this lunatic. In an elegant chamber of the presidential palace, Stilwell met the white mustachioed, medal-laden old man.

"How he looked me over!" recalled Stilwell. "I could feel his eyes reaching into my brain and looking over its cells. He afterward said he was my friend before I had spoken a word."

Though tales have long said that spirit voices implanted the KCM&O in the mind of Stilwell, the fact is that the idea had long been hatching in many heads. Díaz told Stilwell that, in about 1880, former president U. S. Grant had helped organize a railway company using pretty much the same idea. C. P. Huntington, Southern Pacific Railway magnate, had sought a route over the Sierra Madre. President Díaz had a free hand to grant rights and money for a road from Chihuahua to the Pacific, though the Mexican Congress retained the right to approve any other railroad construction. He spoke also of a similar project proposed by Sen. William Windom of Minnesota.

The next morning Díaz sent Stilwell guarantee of concessions plus more than a million dollars of government money to finance building. Stilwell made a deposit of his funds with the Mexican government.

In their talk about previous projects, they had neglected a forerunner of some importance. This was Albert Kimsey Owen, civil engineer, utopian, and major coworker with Senator Windom. A Pennsylvanian, Owen fell in love with Mexico while surveying in the Sierra Madre and along the Gulf of California in 1872. He was fired with the dream of an international, transcontinental railway terminating at the natural harbor of Topolobampo. A social idealist, he organized a number of American Populists, Knights of Labor, Free Silverites, democratic socialists, and other midwestern, progressive working people, who colonized a short-lived utopia near Topolobampo. It was Owen who inspired Senator Windom to build a railway from Topolobampo to Chihuahua, continuing from there to Ojinaga, and then to Piedras Negras, just across the Rio Grande from Eagle Pass.

From Owen's interest arises the only hint of any breach of business ethics on Stilwell's part. An associate said that Stilwell met with Owen many times. In 1911 Owen's widow sued Stilwell for $200,000, charging breach of a written contract between the two men, which she produced in court. The judge found the contract sufficiently vague to deny her motion to bring suit.

After agreements with President Díaz and General Creel, Stilwell's Mexican connection seemed secure. Hidden in it was a budding cancer, however — one of the building contractors was rich Luis Terrazas, practical owner of the state of Chihuahua. A sub-contractor under Terrazas was his avowed enemy, Pancho Villa. Stilwell had awarded Villa and his outfit of twelve teams and scrapers short stretches of two- and three-mile grading. Animosities were to grow.

4.

Progress, Revolution, and Recovery

PLANNING and construction of the Orient proceeded briskly for several years. While volumes have been written of the higher-level financing of the KCM&O, details of planning and financing on community levels are hard to come by. There are a few, however. For instance, any bondholder was to receive, in addition to dividends and other benefits, one cent per mile of road constructed each six months, in the form of a ticket enabling them to ride over the road and select townsite lots to purchase.

There is a saying that the Orient did not build straight from one end to the other or from each end toward the middle — that, rather, it built from each point on the route in opposite directions toward the two outlying points. This misunderstanding may have been introduced by at least one example not correctly interpreted. A section was begun at Blackwell, Texas, building toward San Angelo, and another was started at San Angelo, moving toward Blackwell, on the route to Sweetwater. When the two sections met, a shop man polished the final spike to a silverlike finish. This spike was driven into its tie, securing the final rail and sparking considerable fanfare and speechmaking in the middle of a pasture.

To finance this construction, a hundred-thousand-dollar bonus was demanded of San Angelo citizens, as well as free right-of-way and terminal facilities. When this sum was reduced by half, the demand was met. Though this money raising occurred in 1900, that polished spike was not driven until 1912.

It was in 1910 that Stilwell himself is said to have joined his surveying crew in Irion County west of San Angelo. Mrs. Hattie Hinde and her husband furnished wagons and teams to the crew, and Hattie also provided their meals and hauled the food from their ranch to the ever-changing locations. Often her children rode with her. In the afternoons Hattie drove a wagon loaded with stakes for the surveyors and construction crew until they had worked as far west as Big Lake.

In 1911 the Orient Land Company killed the short-lived Upton County seat of Upland when it created Rankin, the new one. Land involving a townsite was transferred by rancher F. E. Rankin to the Orient Railroad, and in three years Upland was reduced from a population of five hundred souls to only one family, that of the postmaster.

When the rails and the first train finally arrived at Rankin, there was a pleasant celebration for a jubilant crowd. Ranchers were happy in the prospect of shipping cattle by rail, which rescued them from their regular cattle drives to San Angelo — a nine-day journey, going and coming. All present at the first train's arrival were treated to a free ride to a pump station five miles up the line and back home again.

Before 1900 Alpine citizens had expressed desire for a railroad to supplement the Southern Pacific, hoping that freight charges would be reduced by competition and that the town's population would increase. So in 1903 an Orient representative had little trouble in raising $25,000 along with right-of-way and three hundred acres for terminal facilities. Orient rails were still ten years away.

On the Kansas end, so the tale goes, a vision in the night resolved one of Stilwell's major problems. Despite all his success in securing right-of-way, Stilwell could not get permission from the Hannibal and St. Joseph Railway to bridge over its tracks near Kansas City. This crossover was necessary if the Orient ever was to steam into a Kansas City terminal.

Sound asleep, he dreamed of a parcel of land shaped like a piece of pie — a wedge. Trusting his psychic gift, he searched titles and surveys and found it. Indeed, there was a triangular piece of land on the H&SJ line that belonged to nobody. Stilwell promptly made it his own, and with it came the right for the Orient to span his opponent's rails. So the tale was told long ago by the Kansas-born father of Bruce Hackett of Alpine.

Descriptions of construction work are elusive, but some were found in old photographs that show special moments of that gargantuan job.

A pretty young lady in a Gibson-girl hat turns the first shovel of dirt at Emporia, Kansas. Behind her a huge horse-drawn machine is loaded with railroad officials in fedora hats. A few workers are present, and so is the girl's chaperone.

On May 10, 1901, the first spike is driven to launch the Orient in the United States at Anthony, Kansas. A crowd of well-dressed men, women, and children stand around and on a KCM&O locomotive and tender pulling a Missouri Pacific boxcar; by it stand a few workers in overalls. One man is shirtless, revealing his muscular torso. The ties ahead of the locomotive are bare of rails. Black-hooded steam tractors with large, heavily lugged wheels stand behind horses, some of which are hitched to scrapers, some to wagons.

Present is KCM&O president Arthur Stilwell. In his speech he promises that the entire line will be completed to the Pacific coast of Mexico by the end of 1903, one and a half years away. (It finally was, in 1961.)

Near Wichita, like straight, smooth stumps, long rows of bridge pilings are inspected for alignment by civil engineers in white shirts and neckties. Towering over them is the pile driver. The engineers have arrived in a working surrey drawn by a team of mules. Soon the bridge deck will be built and track laid upon it.

Near Maryneal, Texas, between Sweetwater and San Angelo, stands a derricklike pile driver and a track-laying machine called a "Joe Heaver." The track layer resembles an ancient siege tower turned on its side and mounted on a flatcar. The scene is filled with Texas workers in khakis, overalls, and big western hats.

In Mexico construction progressed, and 237 miles of the 637 planned were simultaneously finished from Chihuahua through Creel to the end of the track at Sanchez. Photographs of a magnificent hand-hewn stone masonry culvert in Chihuahua state show that the Mexican engineers and laborers had done superior work. The same cannot always be said of their American counterparts.

In 1906 Orient Construction Camp 106 in the Sierra Madre west of Minaca consists of log cabins built of the abundant Ponderosa pine. One photograph reveals tents, and before them civil engineers in laced boots, Texas hats, and dark shirts. With them are workers in tall, broad-brimmed sombreros.

Gleaming, hand-cut stone piles support a bridge across the Guerrero River. They are not hastily driven creosoted stocks or wooden trestles like those common on the American road.

In July, 1911, the Orient contracted to finish the road from San Angelo to Alpine by December 31, 1912. Prophetically, the first Orient train into Alpine was late. The revolution in Mexico was a major cause of delay, but not the only one.

In 1911 a trap door sprung open under the hopes for the Kansas City, Mexico, and Orient Railroad. The new revolutionary president of Mexico was Francisco Madero, and eighty year old Porfirio Díaz was out. Out with him were the plans of Arthur Stilwell and General Creel.

Pancho Villa had reason to be venomous toward the KCM&O. With his work gang of men, mules, and scrapers, he was a grading subcontractor on the "Oriente." Stilwell, in his genteel attire down in Mexico, is said to have directed the work from his private car. He looked down on Villa, thought him low-class, disliked his sweaty work clothes, never tried to be friendly toward him, and never invited him into the private car.

Furthermore, rich landowner and rancher Luis Terrazas of

Chihuahua offended Villa. He was an Orient contractor over Villa, responsible for grading the line west of Minaca to Creel. When the first sections of the line were completed, there was a fiesta in celebration. Terrazas invited all the subcontractors — except Pancho Villa — to the party.

Though Villa won control of Chihuahua and helped destroy the Terrazas regime, he and other revolutionaries did not do as much damage to Orient properties as to those of other railroads. Nevertheless, Stilwell said, "We had bridges torn down and tracks torn up in 1911 and have been obliged to suspend operations and stop new construction." The Mexico Northwestern suffered as much and more, for locomotives and rolling stock were dynamited and looted. Villa is supposed to have dynamited Stilwell's Sierra Madre silver mine, putting it out of business. This mine is said to have netted $25,000 per month, and Villa could as easily have captured and operated it for his own use. The Orient's general manager for Mexico Juan Treviño wisely moved to El Paso for almost two years while Villa held Chihuahua City.

In 1916 the newly installed Carranza government encouraged a return to business as usual in Mexico. But that didn't stop a group of armed bandits from stopping an Orient train carrying a group of American mining men westward from Chihuahua. The bandits, claiming to be Villistas (but disavowed by Villa), ordered the Americans off the train, lined them up, shot them, and stripped their bodies. One American escaped. Another Orient train soon was dispatched from Chihuahua City to bring back the dead.

On the American side, things went from bad to worse for more mundane reasons. By 1912 the weak roadbed and 75-pound per yard rail were poorly maintained, and trains averaged less than twenty miles per hour. Costly derailments were frequent, and the KCM&O was losing money. In 1912 interest charges on bonds were due, in addition to almost a million dollars that was owed on equipment trust obligations.

It was said, "When Mr. Stilwell runs out of money in railway building, he prays for more and always gets it." But neither

prayer nor anything else worked for him now. He resigned as president of the KCM&O, and his brainchild went into receivership.

Stilwell complained, "Because I had the idea that a railroad was built to serve the people, I was hounded and persecuted. The New York financial interests have been fighting me. For sixteen years I have been followed by detectives. Every friend I meet is handed a note telling him to have nothing to do with me. My only object is to have the Golden Rule dusted off and put back into practice. That's all I ask."

In February, 1913, after a long stay in a California hospital, the despondent Stilwell briefly visited Alpine (which his railway reached one month later). "He wanted to see the Orient extension from San Angelo toward Alpine, a part of the road he had never seen before," said the *Avalanche*. From Alpine he took an auto to Fort Stockton and boarded the Orient he had lost, "traveling from there as an ordinary passenger."

In San Angelo for only a few minutes, he met several friends at the depot there. Memories arose of how, in years before, he "often came to San Angelo in a private Pullman train with many capitalists." In a "pathetic scene," the *Avalanche* reported "he said he was among those who had lost in the game, and that the Morgan financiers had taken the Orient away from him, as they had the Kansas City Southern." Then, "with tears streaming down his cheeks," he said he would settle some business in Kansas City and then was going to Europe, "where men could not be robbed as he had been." Described as "broken hearted and sick," he declared he would "never again live in the United States."

With terrible irony Stilwell, having fallen from power, soon afterward crashed with a plunging elevator, was permanently injured, and lived the rest of his life in pain. Retired, he moved from Kansas City to a New York apartment instead of to Europe, and there he turned to writing.

Other troubles still plagued the Orient. In 1913 a tremendous rainfall in Oklahoma washed out a major long bridge across the South Canadian River. In 1914, five miles north of Alpine—near the o6 and Kimball ranch line, Orient Passenger Train No. 1 was marooned for two days by flash flooding. Passengers were rescued by automobile.

Perhaps the most humbling embarrassment came during World War I when the U.S. government took over all the railroads in the country except one—the Orient. It was of no use to the war effort. Upon request the U.S. Railroad Commission finally allowed the Orient to move empty freight cars. By this time the Orient tracks had reached Alpine, in the middle of the Big Bend, and then they stalled.

In 1913, while the KCM&O suffered, the final spike in Alpine was driven. Most of the story has been assembled by Alpine's historian, Clifford B. Casey.

In December, 1900, the *Alpine Avalanche* stated, "Alpine people are feeling good, for if the Orient crosses the Southern Pacific at Paisano [on the line to Marfa] it can hardly pass up Alpine." Stilwell had announced in 1901 that the rails would reach Topolobampo in 1903, and a citizen wrote the *Avalanche* in 1902, "Dear Mr. Stilwell: Please hurry up that railroad."

In 1903 Alpine understood what was required if the Orient was to consider building there — namely free right of way through Brewster County and a $5,000 cash bonus. The committee that worked with the Orient company included J. D. Jackson, C. A. Brown, W. D. Kincaid, Captain James B. Gillett, Herbert L. Kokernot, Sr., and Judge Wigfall Van Sickle. In 1927 Jackson was named a director of the KCM&O Board.

Construction at Sweetwater started in 1904. The section from there to the Oklahoma line was completed in 1908, and that to San Angelo in 1909. By March, 1910, it had reached Mertzon. Then financial setback delayed completion of the next 132 miles to Girvin, near Fort Stockton, until 1911.

The Orient also graded part of a branch from San Angelo toward Sonora, destination Del Rio. When the Orient gave up on this branch, the Frisco Railroad encouraged local ranchers to build the cattle drive lane from Sonora to the Frisco at Brady. This was a fenced one hundred-mile long, two hundred fifty-foot wide lane with holding pens along the way.

In May, 1911, Alpine people were required to raise another $25,000 to help finance construction of the ninety-six miles from Girvin to Alpine. At first, Orient executives wanted $50,000, but after taking one look at the place and judging the productivity, they settled for half that amount plus about two thousand acres of land. The Orient, having agreed to build the depot a half mile nearer to town than first planned, promised to steam into town by the end of 1912.

The laying of track resumed briskly for a short time. In 1912 Stilwell's financial empire fell apart. In receivership the Orient was refinanced, and again the Joe Heaver track-laying machine lumbered along, and spike hammers clanged away.

In September, 1912, workers had brought the line to within twenty miles of Fort Stockton and were putting down about one and a half miles of track per day. Visiting Alpine, Orient representatives announced that the rails would be there by March,

1913. In the new year, the *Avalanche* ran a weekly report with a diagram showing the progress, until it reported, "March 27, 1913, Orient has reached city limits of Alpine." Big, black headline letters proclaimed:

ALPINE TO CELEBRATE COMPLETION
OF ORIENT RAILROAD APRIL 24 & 25

The KCM&O had arrived — three months late. Not bad, considering that it was thirteen years after Stilwell's first announced completion for the entire road. Five days later, April 1, track was laid and completed to the station building itself.

Alpine was crowing and ready for a fiesta. On April 3 the *Avalanche* said:

FIRST ORIENT TRAIN

While there was no blaring of trumpets, no blowing of whistles nor spilling of "shampoo" water, the Orient railroad was completed to its depot in Alpine — its southern terminus for probably years to come — Tuesday evening.

No silver spike was used to pin down the last rail.

Alpine offers opportunities to the capitalist that will not long remain unaccepted. God has endowed us with a climate that is not excelled anywhere, and there is no reason why Alpine should not be the Denver of Texas.

On April 24 & 25 of this month, Alpine's citizenship expects to have a big celebration in honor of the completion of the Orient. A general invitation is extended to our sister towns to partake of Western hospitality in its true meaning.

WE WANT ALL TO COME

"Thousands of guests," said the *Avalanche*, "were here and all were provided for." An Orient special brought the San Angelo Booster Brigade plus a brass band; the regular puffed in loaded with people from Fort Stockton, Mertzon, and other points. The Southern Pacific brought delegations from El Paso and Marfa to the west, and from San Antonio and Del Rio on the east. In addition hundreds more came from all over the Big Bend country and Permian Basin in autos, buggies, and wagons. Alpine people opened their spare bedrooms to visitors. At the "airdrome" a smoker was held for the men — that is, a beer bust with sandwiches and cigars. The Mountaineers Club entertained the ladies with cookies and punch. That day Alpine players won two baseball games against teams from Fort Stockton and San Angelo. At Friday's barbecue on vacant lots next to the courthouse, eleven beefs and twelve sheep sizzled over the pits.

During the celebration there were two or three dances. The one at the schoolhouse was thrilling for teenager Hallie Crawford — later Stilwell, but no connection with Arthur E. "I was real excited and thought it was grand," Hallie said in later years. "It was the first big dance I'd been to."

Orient passenger trains now rolled all the way between Wichita, Kansas, and Alpine. At Southern Pacific sidings in Alpine, the Orient hooked onto California fruit trains and pulled them to San Angelo for reicing on their journey.

After the line was completed to Presidio in 1930, a regular feature of summer school at Sul Ross State University was the Spanish department's annual tour to Chihuahua on a chartered train. Rails from Chihuahua to Ojinaga had been laid in 1928. The four day excursion could be had, "including round-trip railroad fare, room and meals, for approximately $20," so a university bulletin said. Alpine's Dr. Raymond Wheat, then a student, traveled on at least two of these trips. They were enjoyable, he said, and the only real trouble was a delay of about twenty-six hours in the Mexico desert while workers rebuilt a bridge washed out by a flash flood.

5.

Boom, Bust, and Survival

BEFORE 1930 the Orient almost died. To its receivers, building the section from Wichita to Kansas City proved unfeasible, and its markers, partial roadbed, and few rusting rails were abandoned. Stilwell's prophetic dreams of the pie-shaped plat was in vain. Debt was overbearing. A disastrous two-year drought dragged on in western Texas and Oklahoma. And in 1922 the receivers considered ripping up the entire railroad and selling it for scrap. Then came the miracle.

So the legend goes, in 1921 a Dallas newsman asked Arthur Stilwell if he thought the receivers would forsake his brainchild. He replied with a prophecy from his spirit voices: the Orient would be saved two years hence by gigantic oil discoveries in West Texas.

The miracle came to pass on schedule when Santa Rita No. 1 blew in at Big Lake, which was soon surrounded by countless spouting oil wells in the McCamey area. Rail traffic in oil field equipment boomed, oilmen, and boomtown drifters crowded the passenger cars, and even Alpine shared modestly in the bonanza. Tank cars of drinking water were shipped from Alpine to McCamey, where their cargo is said to have sold for a dollar a gallon, an exaggeration that is the fruit of time. An old-timer said of Big Lake water, "Soap would curdle in it. We used it purely for taking showers." The imported water sold in

Big Lake for two dollars per barrel when the price of oil was exactly half that amount. Worker Oscar Shewmake, who was there, told Dal Herring, "Alpine water was hauled overland about thirty miles from McCamey to Iraan by wagon, and sometimes it sold for about five dollars a barrel. But we drank more home brew than water."

In 1925 the Orient Railroad — with the help of the oil boom — created McCamey when it built a four-mile spur to the drilling site of oilman George B. McCamey. An Orient agent parked a boxcar on the spur, painted "McCamey" on a board, and nailed it to the car. The day after the well came in, a townsite was dedicated, and McCamey soon was known as "The Hub of the Oil Fields." For a time Orient freight agent G. C. Pauley lived with his family in a boxcar on a siding.

The Orient was almost breaking even when rail shipment of crude oil tapered off as oil was transferred to newly completed pipelines. Though saved from destruction, the railroad was put up for sale. Retired Southern Pacific agent J. M. Floyd of Alpine said that the SP had a chance to buy it before it was offered to the Santa Fe. An SP inspector went up and down the tracks and reported, "All that holds the rails together is bermuda grass." So in 1928 the Orient became the Kansas City, Mexico, and Orient branch of the Atchison, Topeka, and Santa Fe, and it was not until 1964 that the Orient became the Santa Fe in name as well as in ownership. The Santa Fe sold Orient holdings in Mexico to a sugar operator and determined immediately to complete the line from Alpine to Presidio and from San Angelo to Sonora. As for the SP, Floyd said, "They shore wished they'd bought it."

At Presidio a bridge across the Rio Grande would connect the Orient with the track at Ojinaga (finished in 1928). In Chihuahua City in 1984, Antonio M. Delgado remembered the hard struggle to build the railroad through and over the vicious desert mountains of North Mexico. His friend Rafael Hermosillo and other young men from Conterosa toiled at two sections north of Falomir and could not endure it for more than a month. They returned home because they were afraid of the terrain and the hard work required.

At the end of 1928 a celebration in Ojinaga was planned for the road's completion, but the fiesta was overshadowed. On December 23, an ill-fated train carried Chihuahua's governor, Gen. Marcelo Caravel toward Ojinaga. A bridge collapsed as the locomotive started over it and the train derailed, killing three crewmen, including the fireman, another friend of Delgado. Though the celebration was cancelled, the Mexican line soon began a regular route to the Rio Grande and awaited its connection to Presidio.

To reach Presidio the Orient would roll from Alpine on leased Southern Pacific tracks to Paisano, from which point new Orient track was to be laid, heading south. In July, 1929, a construction contract was let to Bill List of Kansas City, who prided himself on fast, good work. In August, the first dirt was turned, and work camps came to life in one of the roughest parts of the Big Bend Country.

Few men worked mules to scrapers now. Most drove roaring gasoline tractors, trucks, draglines, and power shovels. Ralph Peters of Alpine saw an excavator digging borrow ditches and piling up dirt to be graded for a roadbed. This machine carved slices of earth five miles long without stopping.

Men welcomed the jobs, because the Great Depression had begun. Workers a-plenty could be hired locally and also from the migrants gathered at the SP stockpen near Marfa. Freight trains were crowded with job seekers. Jack Hord of Alpine once heard that Jess Willard, world heavyweight boxing champion from 1915 to 1919, operated a machine on the project after his big money had played out.

Patricio Navarette, known in Alpine as "Picho," was one of the workmen. He was paid $2.50 per ten-hour day, plus meals and a bunk in a "circus train" camp car. In one of the other cars, Picho said, there was a shower for bathing. Twenty years old at the time, Picho was a strong, hard worker who tamped ties and carried and laid rails. There were 150 men on that job, Picho said, none here illegally, and he did not remember anyone being seriously injured. Food in the camp kitchen was good, and the cook, Eleno Cano, called Leno, later owned one of the best restaurants in Alpine.

J. W. Allhands, a subcontractor, described the building of the seventy-three-mile Presidio section. Men drove nine Caterpillar power shovels and two draglines across pasture and desert and up and down mountains as far as sixty miles ahead of a rail point. Sometimes they climbed almost straight up, the men shoving and pulling levers, making the way sure for their tracks by scooping out in front and dumping behind.

Though much of the going was easy, it became hard when they hit rock. Sometimes a man jostled with an air hammer at one hundred pounds pressure for hours to drill a three-foot hole, with another man constantly passing him sharp steel. The air hammer pounded day and night in conjunction with the battering jackhammers and the ring of anvils.

The "powder monkeys" had to scratch their heads. Some shots by these dynamite workers scarcely disturbed the rock, and a variety of recipes was called for — shots of two, ten, forty, and even ninety sticks of dynamite. On mountainsides men dug big "coyote holes" for storing large amounts of explosives.

Perhaps one of the biggest construction blasts up to that time was a hair-raising shot of ten thousand pounds of black powder and five hundred pounds of dynamite. The ground shook for miles around as the explosion jarred thirty-five hundred cubic yards of rock from a 128-foot slice on a mountain slope. A fifteen hundred-cubic-yard boulder rolled out of the gash and rumbled down into a creek bed.

Alamito Creek provided plenty of water for the men, the camps, and the engineering work. The track bridges the Alamito five times between Paisano and Presidio. In fear of flash floods, bridge men would work all night, excavating sometimes forty feet down for a foundation, setting forms, mixing concrete, and pouring it.

As the line approached Presidio, bosses and workers sought

relief from Prohibition in the cantinas of Ojinaga. Many returned to work with hangovers and sore arms, having been vaccinated for smallpox by immigration officers.

Now that the road had come to the Rio Grande all the way from Wichita, Kansas, the international railroad bridge was built, twenty-two hundred feet long with nine hundred stocks of piling. At first the Mexican government insisted that 80 percent Mexican labor be employed after the bridge reached the middle of the Rio Grande. This requirement, however, was soon modified.

In November, 1930, the special train of officials passed through Alpine and arrived in Presidio to celebrate the event. The last ceremonial spike was driven by Luis L. León, representing the president of Mexico, Ortíz Rubio.

The depot was located quite a distance from old Presidio, in effect almost creating a new town. The tale goes that somebody asked an Orient official, "Why did you build the station so far from Presidio?"

The answer was, "So it would be near the railroad."

The Santa Fe had inherited the projected depot and bridge sites and town lots around them along the entire Orient system. It was Arthur Stilwell's custom to cash in on real estate in connection with his establishment of rail points. Land promotion in Presidio stepped up, and Orient employees were offered building lots in Presidio at reduced prices.

Sick and aging, Arthur E. Stilwell would not live to know that his dream of international commerce and cooperation was fulfilled in its own way. While in New York, his interest in spiritualism and Christian Science increased. He corresponded with Sir Arthur Conan Doyle, wrote books about his rise and fall in business, and planned a series of novels dictated by spirit voices. In September, 1928, he died, at age sixty-nine. A month later his wife Jenny leapt to her death from a window of their twelfth story apartment. Her note read, "I just couldn't live without my loved one."

In the opinion of the late Dennis Brown, Santa Fe agent in Alpine, American forces worked to inhibit completion of the "Oriente" in Mexico. He observed in 1957 that Topolobampo has a year-round growing season, with a half-million acres of rich truck and fruit land. Therefore, it was in the interest of the California Fruit Growers Association, he said, to block Santa Fe's completion of the road to its projected terminus. When Stilwell started the road, Imperial Valley was still a desert. Also, Brown said, "The Santa Fe was not keen on completing the road, because it would put the Santa Fe in competition with itself." The freight rates through Mexico and on the Santa Fe in Texas both were much cheaper than the Santa Fe rate across the Rocky Mountains — one of the highest rates in the country. Consequently, Mexican fruit and vegetables and Ponderosa lumber were "protected" out. Halibut and other fish caught and canned at Topolobampo Bay had to be shipped to California instead of Presidio to be distributed to inland America. Brown also observed that if the "Oriente" were finished, importers could save five days of rail freight by receiving their Asian goods at Topolobampo.

Though it could not serve its original purpose, during the 1950s the Orient seemed to be at least breaking even. The cars transported cattle from many points, oil from and equipment to Big Lake and Rankin, and ore from Mexico. There was traffic in gypsum from Hamlin and cement from the plant at Maryneal. Marathon and Marfa cattle came to Alpine for shipment north on the Orient, and one of the great autumn events at Alpine was the cattle drive from Herbert Kokernot's o6 Ranch to the loading pens near town. When town people heard the cattle bawling, many drove out to the pens to watch the excitement, taking their children with them. The Orient should have been more prosperous, Dennis Brown believed, but, "his own agents and other Orient people stole Stilwell out," apparently by taking money from the till that should have gone to the company.

In 1940, when Mexico nationalized its railroads, about 150 miles of the "Oriente," crossing the Sierra Madre and dropping down about two thousand feet, were not finished. American engineers, surveying over the mountain tops, had never worked out a feasible plan for making the descent. About 1945, engineer Francisco Togño routed the line along the tortuous bottom of the three thousand-foot deep canyon. Here the scenery ranks with the most spectacular in the world and includes La Barranca del Cobre ("Copper Canyon"), six thousand feet deep and much larger than Arizona's Grand Canyon. In the fifteen miles beyond La Barranca there are sixty tunnels and many bridges. One stretch of five miles has ten tunnels and five bridges. In another one-and-a-half miles of linear distance, there are four-and-a-half miles of winding track. The longest tunnel runs 1.2 miles; the longest bridge is 1,454 feet in length, the tallest, three hundred feet in height. At one point the rails tunnel under a two hundred-foot waterfall.

In 1961 the Chihuahua al Pacifico came out of the Sierra Madre, crossed the hundred miles of coastal plain, and puffed onto a dock at Topolobampo's bay on the Gulf of California.

In the 1980s the Santa Fe saw traffic increase on the Big

Bend's Orient line. During a grain embargo against Russia, about four hundred cars of grain per week came down from midwestern elevators to pass through the Big Bend to Mexico. There much of it was sold to the embargoed country. Not as much ore was hauled out of Mexico and across the Big Bend as had been, but a few commodities came through, such as tomato paste for making ketchup. Also, some hope was attached to prospects of oil development south of the Rio Grande.

In 1981 the Santa Fe suggested to the Texas State Railroad Commission that stations at Alpine, Fort Stockton, and Big Lake be closed. Mertzon, Rankin, McCamey, and others were shut down long before. Trainmen were laid off as the regional office at San Angelo computerized freight handling and provided a computer card with every waybill. By reading these cards, the conductor could spot each car in terms of siding, warehouse, and dock. Switching was handled by train crews. The vital station at Presidio's international bridge remained open.

While the economic slump of the 1980s was setting in, the year 1981 was one of Santa Fe's most profitable. As in the depression year of 1930, Santa Fe improved and built on its Orient line, for instance by installing flashing signals at highway and street crossings. In 1982 workmen laid thousands of new ties and a thousand tons of rock between Fort Stockton and Alpine. Plans called for new and heavier rail to replace the old by 1985. Alpine agent Bill Roberts said, "I think that Santa Fe anticipates good business down here. Otherwise they wouldn't be spending that kind of money."

By 1990, however, the new rail had not been laid, the Alpine station was closed, and traffic fell to one train a week between San Angelo and Presidio. Then there were none, and the Presidio Depot was abandoned and locked.

Word got around that Santa Fe was about to abandon the 360-mile run from San Angelo to Presdio and sell its rails and equipment for scrap. With scores of jobs and a cherished tradition about to vanish, the locals rallied. In July, State Senator Bill

Sims and State Representative Robert Junell called a public meeting. Santa Fe officials cited loss of revenue because of the "oil-bust" and the closing of the sulphur mine at Fort Stockton.

An identical fate seemed in store for almost all of the Orient. In August and September, Foard County Judge Charlie Bell called meetings at the court house in Crowell to organize "a united opposition to the proposed abandonment of the Santa Fe Railroad between Sweetwater, Texas, and Cherokee, Oklahoma (on the Kansas border)." County judges put the case to U.S. Senator Phil Gramm, who pressed the Interstate Commerce Commission to save the Old Orient because of its importance to the regional economy and to international trade. "This line," Gramm said, "is the only feeder line that runs from Northwest Mexico to Topolobampo," and to abandon it "could stifle the national goal of increased commerce."

In October a Santa Fe official declared that no abandonment petition had been filed; rather, "sale of the line to a short-line operator is likely before the end of the year." Digressing, he objected to criticism of Santa Fe's actions by Agriculture Commissioner Jim Hightower and other public officials. Hightower publicized a study to show how farmers along the route would be hampered if it shut down. Senator Sims and Representative Junell then called another public meeting to urge that the old Orient keep rolling.

Nevertheless, by November the Orient rails again seemed fated for the junk pile. In November, Santa Fe announced the sale of "the last remaining segments of the old Kansas City, Mexico and Orient Railway to an individual associated with a salvage firm," according to John Walker in the San Angelo *Standard-Times*. They sold three segments of track in Texas and Oklahoma to Orient Railcorp, based in Conroe, Texas, a firm not listed with the Texas secretary of state but "affiliated with Continental Rail Co., an assumed name for Illinois-based IBS, Inc., a railroad scrapper." The manager of this firm was an employee of Continental Rail. Each time Walker tried to contact Orient Railcorp, he was greeted by an answering machine.

After speaking to a representative of Continental Rail, Representative Junell said, "I advised him that if he intended to come down here and start to scrap this line, he would have one tough fight on his hands."

More county judges and business and civic leaders entered the fray. Typical is the letter of Brewster County Judge Tom Connor (Alpine) to the Interstate Commerce Commission. In his opposition to the sale, Judge Connor pointed out, "Orient Railcorp has not at any time operated a railroad line for profit." Because of the "presumed certainty of a free-trade agreement between Mexico and the United States," he intimated, the rails to the international bridge at Presidio should be kept in place.

Soon, a solution seemed possible if not imminent: creation of the multi-county South Orient Rural Transportation District. This was an eleven-county entity stretching from Coleman through San Angelo, McCamey, Fort Stockton, and Alpine to Presdio.

In early December, 1990, the district became a reality, and suddenly the sale of the Orient to a scrapper was on hold. A Santa Fe vice-president said, "There has been a tremendous amount of political upheaval in Texas about this"; and a Santa Fe lawyer observed, "The public officials have spoken and Santa Fe officials have heard their message."

(Nevertheless, some sections of track between San Angelo and the Kansas line became bare roadbed, the rails removed. The KCM&O, as Arthur E. Stilwell imagined it, was no more — it was now a series of disjointed segments.)

Time passed while funding by private investment matched with state funds made it possible for the South Orient Rail Transportation District to buy the route. Of the $5.5 million required to buy the route, $3.5 million took the form of a state grant, while the remaining $2.5 million was raised by South Orient Railroad, Ltd., a Dallas-based group of investors and leaseholders. Rail Operators, Inc., would run the operation.

Consequently, on a bright March day in 1992 a crowd of more than two hundred gathered outside Alpine's Orient depot for the same reason they had done so in May, almost eighty years before.

"Here she comes!"— characteristically late, a Diesel locomotive and two passenger cars of dignitaries on the South Orient's maiden run. At Alpine, as at Fort Stockton and Presidio, the stops were filled with welcomes, responses, speeches, music, and refreshments.

For weeks thereafter Big Bend people could see nothing either moving or stationary on the South Orient track. Then the reborn carrier was hauling ten cars on one round-trip a week to the Rio Grande. By June the number of cars went to twenty, and then to forty. A second weekly train was added. In one August week she pulled thirty cars out of San Angelo, to leave seven of them at Rankin. A haulage arrangement with Burlington Northern Railway made a "boomlet" possible. "They were the only major Western railroad," said Claude Griggs, general manager of Rail Operators, Inc., "that doesn't have a ground link to Mexico." His company runs the trains on the South Orient.

Griggs hoped even to expand the South Orient by acquiring Santa Fe tracks from Brownwood to Fort Worth. He expected Alpine to profit more, though modestly, than other small towns on the South Orient. By September, 1992, train crews were already staying overnight in Alpine, and plans foresaw placing a switching crew in residence there.

The South Orient expected to be hauling sand (for drilling operations at Rankin), wood chips, and grain such as oats and milo to Presidio and Mexico. Delivery of lumber, mining products, and intermodel containers also was contemplated.

Old-timers in the Big Bend chuckle as they remember days of the "Old Orient Railroad."

Big Bend rancher Hallie Stillwell told how she filed a claim against the Orient for their mishandling a shipment of her steers. Even though a railroad is obligated to provide some water, feed, and comfort to the animals, many of Hallie's arrived at their destination starved, dehydrated, and freezing, and some were dead. The marketability of the surviving cattle was damaged.

"I complained," she said, "and it took them the longest time to get ready to settle." About nine o'clock one morning she met with an Orient representative in Lubbock.

Hallie simply described her bunch of cattle, with an account of their abused condition, and asked for what she considered a fair settlement. This took her only a few minutes.

The Orient man listened to her brief, then piled a stack of papers on his desk with detailed accounts of every single cow in Hallie's several carloads. The morning dragged on as he discussed them one by one and said something about what the KCM&O considered a decent reimbursement for each.

"Well," said Hallie, "by the time he had gone through all

that I felt only a foot high. I just knew I wasn't going to get anything at all like what I thought it would be fair to ask for."

At last the Orient man finished, and Hallie said, "By this time I feel about like a wet Mexican. Just give me my 'checky.'"

The Orient man tilted back in his swivel chair, roared with laughter, and said, "Come on. I'll take you to lunch."

At a restaurant he said, "Mrs. Stillwell, you used an expression I never heard before. What is a 'wet Mexican'?"

Hallie was stunned by this gap in the man's knowledge. When she explained, he laughed again. He was obviously not a Texan, or he would have been familiar with the practice of undocumented Mexican workers entering the United States illegally by crossing the Rio Grande into Texas.

Back at the Orient office, the claims man promptly made out a check to Hallie for every penny she asked for in the first place.

Glen Burgess, formerly of Alpine, likes to tell how he once became a sort of hero to his fellow travelers on the Ojinaga-Chihuahua run. In winter sometime in the 1950s, the coach was warm and the windows closed. Burgess was talking and drinking beer with two or three of the Mexican passengers who complained that their beer was warm. Finding a bit of stout cord, Burgess hung several bottles out the window in the icy air. In a short while the beer was delightfully potable, and his newfound friends complimented him extravagantly for his ingenuity.

About 1939 along those same tracks in Mexico, a poker game was heating up. Rancher Henry Richardson was losing money, got mad, and threw the cards out the window. He called for a new deck as the old cards blew and danced along the rails behind the train. There was no new deck.

The game seemed all over to the other players, also of Brewster County — Zeb Decie, Clay Holland, Joe Hord, Gay Meriwether, J. C. Weston, and Gene Benson. (That is the roster of roving gamblers as recalled by Ray LaBeff and the late Jack Hord of Alpine.)

Richardson addressed the conductor and the other passengers. "Stop the train!" he said. "I'll pay a dollar a card for every one anybody can find. On top of that I'll give five dollars more to whoever finds the most."

The train screeched to a halt, backed up, and stopped. Men scrambled after the cards on the right of way. They recovered every one of the fifty-two, Richardson paid up, and the trainful of convivial men rode on to Chihuahua.

Several tales of the "Old Orient" were told by V. J. Smith. Northeast of Alpine, Hovey was sometimes a busy station, especially at cattle-shipping time. The Hovey agent had been bawled out by faraway bosses because of his nonconformity to rules. Consequently, a train dispatcher in San Angelo received a clicking telegraphic message from him on his key: "Bull chasing brakeman in direction of Alpine. Please wire instructions."

"Old Orient" train crews were accommodating, according to stories that are told. A lady's hat blew out the window, a conductor stopped the train, backed it up, and rescued the millinery. I myself experienced the Orient's accommodations to its passengers. When I was traveling from Chihuahua for Topolobampo, the conductor stopped our train and backed up about a half mile to retrieve the baby bottles and other infant gear a tourist couple had left behind on the station platform.

Smith said he was once on a "doodlebug" passenger car — rather like a motorized streetcar — in which a collector of desert plants was riding. The conductor obligingly halted the train and helped the naturalist pull interesting specimens on the right of way.

Another conductor made a lecture tour of the run from Alpine to San Angelo. Smith said one of his encomiums caused a lady to remark, "My lands! I was going to get off here at Mertzon, but the way he talked, I thought we was at Atlantic City." The same conductor named Holy Mountain, just east of where the Alpine–Fort Stockton highway crosses the Orient tracks. He named it for the arrangement of its vegetation, which formed an uncertain "H" followed by "OLY". Without success, he tried to talk Orient workmen into climbing up to transplant and straighten out the H.

One of the conductors is said to have served as the Hovey school teacher. When the train stopped, he walked to the schoolhouse, checked his pupil's progress, and assigned lessons. Then he collected papers, which he graded during the Orient's leisurely progress up and down the line.

The legendary courtesy of Orient trainmen was remembered from the girlhood of Florence Forchheimer Halpern of Alpine. When the freight and passenger train to Fort Stockton paused for water at Hovey, she and other passengers walked across the road to the ranch provision store of the Graef Brothers, who were ranchers themselves. The conductor patiently held the train until the people finished their little shopping and much visiting. Florence especially enjoyed drawing her own root beer from a keg-shaped machine and sipping it as the mountains and greasewood crept by the car windows.

In another tale a cowman on his way to Chancellor suggested to the conductor: "Those shop boys in San Angelo ought to unhitch the cowcatcher from the front end and wire it onto the rear end. We ain't liable to catch up with no cows, but what's to stop them from walkin' in the back door?"

In the San Angelo station the train bulletin is supposed to have read:

SANTA FE — 3 hours late, account washout

ORIENT — on time, cause unknown

Yet another yarn tells of a man who asked to buy a round-trip ticket at the Presidio depot ticket window. The agent asked, "Where to?" The traveler replied, "Why, back here, of course!"

The dream railroad of Arthur E. Stilwell may have died, but the friendly spirit of Big Bend people and the train crews lived on. It seems that the very memory of such folk traditions — and the many tales — fueled the sentiment that found ways and money to keep the cars rolling on the South Orient. In September, 1992, at the Alpine depot, engineer Jim Fogleman said, "The people along the route have been just great to us."

And the *Alpine Avalanche* advised its readers, "The South Orient leaves Alpine for Presidio around 8 to 8:30 A.M. Tuesdays and Fridays, and leaves for San Angelo at the same time on Wednesdays and Saturdays. The crews appreciate the friendliness of Alpine residents who come out to wave them on."

PART III
Raids across the Border

6.

Bandits in the Big Bend

BIG BEND settlers and their families were jumpy. The tag ends of war were about to roar across the Rio Grande into Texas. After 1910 Mexico was convulsed in revolution, and by mid-1911 U.S. Cavalry patrols scouted the desert flats and the twisting trails through mountains and canyons — trails where thieves could hide. With their headquarters in Marfa, contingents were stationed at Alpine and Marathon.

Many North Mexican families were desperate for necessities: food, clothing, bedding, household articles, and tools. Guerrilla fighters craved guns and horses. While many Texas — Mexican and Anglo — were bandit victims, a few were collaborators. Some, both Mexican and Anglo, sold weapons and provisions to "revolutionaries" and would shield them from capture. Often coworkers and kinsmen, they all were neighbors.

In the Big Bend, this "near war" flared up first in Brewster County, though it came to encompass the area from Boquillas, up the Rio Grande through the Chisos, the Chinatis, and the Sierra Vieja, to Fort Hancock. The biggest and most deadly raid in the Big Bend struck Glenn Springs in May, 1916. Before and after, however, there were countless thefts, often miscalled "raids," that drew taut the cords of anxiety.

Especially skittish were J. O. Langford at Hot Springs and Jesse Deemer at his store a few miles down the river. In 1909

Langford moved with his wife, Bessie, and two small daughters onto his newly bought riverbank land. Here he built his stone house and trading post and also formed a sharecropping agreement with a neighboring farmer, Cleofas. Ambitiously, he developed a health resort, because the hot spring water that gushed into the adjacent Rio Grande was invigorating and thought to be a cure for several diseases. The family expected a modestly prosperous future in the wild setting they loved.

Regarded by some as eccentric, the native German Deemer was a mining engineer who had spent many years in Mexico, where he held some useful friendships. By 1912 he was associated with the silver mine at Boquillas, Mexico. Assisted by Pablo Acala, he and Louie Ritchey of Marathon owned a trading post in Texas, located at the place known today as Rio Grande Village. Suspicions arose concerning some active disloyalty of Deemer toward the United States but these surely were unfounded.

Just as Langford's health camp was breaking even, talk of banditry and violence nearby in Mexico drifted across the Rio Grande to alarm the fee-paying campers and health bathers. They had heard about Los Banderos Colorados—"Red Flaggers," whose banner was said to mean that they killed all captives. In 1912 Langford heard that the Red Flaggers had hit Ojinaga, made off with a bunch of cattle, and shot every man who stood up to them.

Shortly after that, news came. A lad barely large enough to clamber onto his burro rode up and told Langford of new trouble across the river. Bandits were on their way to this place, he said, and his terrified neighbors were bringing into Texas all their valuables, horses, and cattle. Many, he said, already had hidden themselves in the Dead Horse Mountains and the Chisos. Langford thought, "What is there to prevent the raiders from following them into Texas? Nothing."

Rewarded with cookies, the youngster ambled away on his burro, and Langford cleaned his guns. Then he rallied his customer guests, who loaded wagons and hacks to move from their scattered campsites to fortify the Langford house, a sturdy building of stone.

As sleepless men guarded windows and doors or posted as sentries, the night passed quietly. After daybreak horses drew a wheeled procession away to Marathon, taking with it Langford's main source of income. Though Langford begged his wife to take their two little girls and get out, she refused. She would stay and share in the plight.

For several nights Langford, his dog Tex, and Cleofas stood watch in a draw about a hundred yards from the house. Cleofas was unconcerned about the safety of his own family, because he believed that bandits would pillage only Anglos and not Mexicans on the Texas side of the river. Both men kept .30-.30 rifles ready, and Langford also armed himself with a pistol and a shotgun.

Late the second night, Tex stood, growled, and bristled, glaring into the dark toward the Rio Grande. The screeching laugh of barn owls was the only sound. The breath of both men stopped at the stumbling splash of horses in the shallow river and the creaking of saddle leather. About fifteen shadowy riders crossed into Texas. As Langford gripped Tex's muzzle, he was frightened but determined to fight if need be.

At the mouth of Tornillo Creek the riders stopped, walked their horses aimlessly about, chattered Spanish to each other, and then rode back into Mexico.

For three more nights, Langford, Cleofas, and Tex stood their watch. Then came word that the Mexican villages of Boquillas and San Vicente had been plundered. After killing several men, the thieves had ridden back to their hideout in the San Vicente Mountains.

Alarmed, Langford and the neighboring Deemer sought help. They rode to Marathon, where they begged the cavalry commander to place a detachment close to them. Under Lt. James L. Collins, twenty-five men set up camp at Lanoria, a few miles north of Hot Springs and Deemer's store. This place was the only village on the Old Ore Road, along which wagons hauled fluorspar to the railroad at Marathon from the Puerto Rico mine near Boquillas. With cavalry patrols now "riding the river" to intimidate marauders, Big Bend settlers could almost relax.

The cavalry was assisted by tighter border control enforced by mounted U.S. Customs inspectors, or "river guards." Mexican nationals could cross the river only at specified points and at certain hours of the day. Violators were hauled to Alpine and put on a train to El Paso for deportation to Juárez, from there to find their own way home.

One exception was ten-year-old Feliz Díaz, who innocently waded the river one day to look for a job herding goats. When river guards wagoned him away to Alpine with other Mexican nationals "somebody with a little sense," said Langford, held onto him. For several days the delighted lad was the honored guest of local lawmen, who took him around to marvel at the store windows, electric lights, and daily arrival of several passenger trains. He ate well. In a few days immigration officers brought him back to the Langfords', where they watched him splash toward home in the hills of Mexico.

A single day in 1913 brought two thunderbolts of bad news. President Madero had been killed, sparking all-out revolutionary, guerrilla war. Worse, a sergeant brought Lieutenant Collins's message to Langford that the Lanoria detachment was pulling out to Marathon for possible foreign service. Outgoing President Taft planned to concentrate ten thousand troops at Galveston, bracing for possible war against Mexico if his elected successor, Woodrow Wilson, chose to pursue it. The later rumor that the troops left because Jesse Deemer was angry at the soldiers and insisted on their withdrawal seems baseless.

The Langfords' fate was settled. They closed their store and tourist camp, shut up their home, and moved to El Paso. "Don't cry, Bessie," Langford said to his wife. "We'll be back just as soon as this trouble is over." They came back fourteen years later, in 1927.

Some of the first "raids"— or nonviolent robberies of 1913 — seem to have occurred not near the Rio Grande, but near Alpine. There was, of course, trouble elsewhere along the border from the Gulf of Mexico to the Pacific.

On Saturday or Sunday, February 15 or 16, said the *Alpine Avalanche*, "Mexican bandits raided the ranch of Lee Hancock, fourteen miles north of Alpine." Taken from the place were five good horses, two saddles, four guns, and ammunition. About twenty miles south of town, the Lawrence Haley ranch was robbed, and saddles, bridles, and other articles were stolen. Somewhere in the vicinity about seventy beefs were driven off.

Brewster County Sheriff Allen Walton pulled together a posse and picked up a horseback trail. In the posse were locally well-known characters, such as former Texas Ranger Julius Caesar Bird, John Young, and Anja—called "Angie"—Wilson. "As the

Mexicans are known to be bad men and are armed to the teeth," said the local paper, "there has been much uneasiness felt about those who are pursuing them." About fifty miles south of Alpine, the robbers were seen by James Cotter, near his Green Valley ranch, heading south.

On Thursday Sheriff Walton called to Alpine from one of the few ranches with a telephone that "the Mexican thieves crossed the river about an hour ahead of his posse." Lawmen concluded that the robbers must have been hired hands who were in Texas illegally and decided to go back to Mexico, perhaps joined by a few restless local men.

Fear of bandits shook Alpine, Marfa, and Valentine. The Marfa Commercial Club secretary told J. D. Jackson, president of the Alpine club, how the local soldiers had been ordered to pull out for Galveston. On February 19 Jackson and Brewster County Judge A. M. Turney wired Gov. O. B. Colquitt that either troops or Texas Rangers were required immediately.

Within a week the governor reassured the Big Bend by wiring Sheriff Walton to deputize as many men as he needed to protect his people. About the same time, U.S. Sen. Morris Sheppard telegraphed Judge Turney, asking him how many troops he thought would do. On February 24 the judge told Senator Sheppard that the troop pullout would leave four hundred miles of the Rio Grande exposed to danger, and at least a thousand soldiers were "urgently needed" to be stationed at Boquillas, Polvo (now Redford), and settlements between Alpine and the river. The Terrell County sheriff at Sanderson, sixty-five miles east, said there had been no bandit trouble around there.

Before the end of that frightening February, the bandit scare slacked off. At its height the bandit news made only the inside pages of the *Avalanche.* For several weeks the front-page feature was a box charting the approaching tracks of the Kansas City, Mexico, and Orient Railway—the "Old Orient." In the coming weeks Alpine gave all its energy to entertaining more than a thousand guests who would arrive on special trains from a dozen towns. There was little time for bandits when Alpine's hour of long-anticipated prosperity seemed at hand.

According to the *Avalanche,* the governor grew tired of "waiting on the federal government to furnish protection" and "ordered four troops of the Texas State Guard to the border." He was prepared, he said, to call out the entire state guard if need be. Also, the governor bolstered the Texas Ranger force to eighty men, there being at the time only fifteen Rangers in the state. Then the governor sent his newly mobilized force not to the Big Bend but to Brownsville. As it turned out, the Big Bend got nothing from Governor Colquitt's promise, and many people were resentful. Despite local frustration, the *Avalanche* defended the governor's good intentions.

For Alpine it was back to business as usual, in hopes that

business would pick up with the new railroad. Bandits from Mexico? Maybe they would stay on their side of the river.

But some of them did not. By 1915 thieving bands plundered ranches and rural homes with regularity. When Gov. James E. Ferguson pleaded with President Wilson for troops in the Big Bend, only a handful were sent. Near Alpine in March, 1916, four bandits almost wrecked a train, but were captured by wary soldiers.

Two months later violent destruction and killing traumatized the Big Bend. In May it was not ranchers, but businessmen and their families along with workers and soldiers who were assaulted in a triple bandit attack. First the outlaws destroyed and looted much of Glenn Springs, killing three soldiers and a small boy. Next, they pillaged Jesse Deemer's store near the head of Boquillas Canyon, kidnapping Deemer and two other men. Finally, they robbed the mine store across the river near Boquillas and kidnapped perhaps seven men there. Some of the Glenn Springs–Boquillas raiders seem to have been Texan collaborators.

Though not nearly as destructive and murderous as the raid on Columbus, New Mexico, a month earlier, these attacks were among the most terrifying of all the border raids — especially the one on Glenn Springs.

7.

The Glenn Springs Horror

NO PLACE could seem more drowsy and peaceful than Glenn Springs did in 1916. By a running, spring-fed creek, the village and a nine-man cavalry camp stood south of the Chisos on the shrubby desert, about twenty miles from the Rio Grande. Mountains reached skyward on all sides.

Smoke rose from stacks above the boiler shed, and in a series of vats, boiling water with carbolic acid separated the commercially useful wax from bundles of wild-growing *candelilla*. Near the wax-rendering vats was the company store. It was managed by C. G. Compton, who lived in a house close by with his three small children: a nine-year-old girl and two small boys, one of whom was deaf and mute. Expecting a baby, Mrs. Compton was away at Marathon. A short distance farther west was the house of newly wed C. K. Ellis and his bride. Ellis, who had an artificial leg, was partner in the wax business with "Cap" C. D. Wood. Scattered about were a few *jacals* — dwellings for Mexican laborers, many with families — their pack burros strolling loose.

Several pyramidal tents had housed a detachment of Troop A, 14th Cavalry Regiment, but the men now occupied only one. Near the corral the camp's small adobe cook house was roofed with sheet metal thickly overlaid with dry, boiled-out *candelilla* weed. Meant to cool the shack's interior, this roof would become the worst horror of the impending bandit raid.

The home of Cap Wood and his family looked down from

a south Chisos slope called "Robber's Roost," about a mile and a half west of Glenn Springs (four miles by the road leading to it). On the day before the raid, Wood took his wife, Julia, and their small son to Alpine because of ominous rumors. Capt. Casper W. Cole, Troop A Commander, reported that he had heard "that a band of Villa bandits [had] assembled about 150 miles south and east of Ojinaga for the purpose of attacking Presidio or the Chisos Mines [Terlingua]."

Accounts of this story come mainly from three sources — Compton, the soldiers, and Cap Wood. These are both enhanced and muddled by newspaper stories and legends from the time.

It was Friday, May 5, Cinco de Mayo — Mexico's festive independence day. Storekeeper Compton said, "We expected a raid that very night. It was rumored that they were going to shoot up Terlingua, but they didn't. They attacked Glenn Springs and Boquillas and carried Mr. Deemer off into Mexico with 'em. That's about twenty-three miles away — right on the river — not over a mile from it."

The warnings of these rumors could not prevent a tragic mistake that contributed to the Glenn Springs debacle. A number of well-equipped Cavalry reinforcements with at least one truck were to roll into Glenn Springs several hours before the attack. But the contingent made an unscheduled halt, camped for the night, and knew nothing of the raid until the next day. It must be remembered that there was no telephone connection, much less telegraph or wireless, out of the southernmost Big Bend country. Messages traveled only by hand carrier.

Several stories, not always consistent, tell of what happened that night.

Legends say that about eleven o'clock somebody knocked on Compton's door. One version says that when he opened the door, he faced several armed men. Another, however, says that it was only one unarmed Mexican. Yet another says that the caller or callers wore masks. Supposedly they (or he) asked how many soldiers were camped there. Some say that Compton, caught unaware, said, "Nine"; others say that he was suspicious and replied, "None."

The *Alpine Avalanche* reported a few days later that Compton had sensed something suspicious. Though his own dog barked at the approach, he had heard none of the village dogs make a sound. It was said that the masks concealed the identity of men Compton knew, having sold them beans and tobacco across the counter. He must have known that some of his Mexican neighbors were *partideros* (partisans), sympathetic with one or the other violent revolutionary cause, and also that many more were loyal Texans who would have nothing to do with the warring factions.

At a congressional investigation hearing three years later, Compton said, "That night there were only three Mexican families in their quarters. They were nearly all off visiting different places." Seeming also to contradict these stories, he said, "A bunch of Mexican bandits ran in there that night about eleven o'clock and began to shoot things up immediately." At the hearing he said nothing about anybody knocking on his door, nothing about masks, nothing about dogs.

At least one popular writer has depicted the invaders riding into the settlement, yelling wildly, and blasting away with their guns from horseback. On the contrary, as Captain Cole reported, "The bandits made the attack dismounted, having left their horses under cover some distance away, and attacked from three sides, north, west, and south, and at a distance varying from 30 feet to 200 yards." The captain's report agrees with that of Compton.

The raiders must have planned to kill the soldiers, burn the *candelilla* works, steal all the horses they could find, and plunder the store and houses.

"From the meager information we had," said Captain Cole, the cavalry knew "the bandits were made up of both Carranzistas and Villistas with a considerable number of Mexicans from this side of the river." Apparently unified from desperation, some bandits yelled, "Viva Villa!" and others, "Viva Carranza!" Rumors persisted, however, that Pancho Villa was the responsible instigator.

Yet another legend, according to Frances Springfield of Marathon, says that before the bandits arrived, the Ellis couple, Compton, and Compton's Mexican hired woman were sitting under the arbor in front of the Ellis house. The Compton children were in bed.

Suddenly, chaos erupted as shooting started, and Compton's house (according to legend) was set ablaze (actually, it was not), as was the wax plant. The Mexican woman ran for Compton's little girl to carry her to safety. Before the boys could get out of the house, a bandit killed one of them. Compton, so says the tale, took off alone to the hills. Mrs. Ellis fled, and her husband, who had removed his wooden leg to rest, hobbled over the rocks and cactus on his stump, reducing it to a bloody mass. The Ellis couple, as Mrs. Springfield heard it, found refuge in the John Rice home. So goes the story. Legends like this, born in gossip, seem to enhance the truth with melodrama, pathos, grisly detail, and tragedy.

Actually, when shooting began, the terrified Ellis and his wife first ran to hide in a canyon back of their home, then walked twelve miles to the John Rice ranch house, a grueling hike for a man with a wooden leg. As for Compton, according to his own narrative, he was indoors with his children and stayed there as long as possible.

But what about the soldiers?

At the corral a sentry watched while his relief man was resting nearby. Only these two were in uniform. Seven of the men, including their leader, Sgt. Charles E. Smyth, were sound asleep in their BVD's.

Sergeant Smyth and one other man slept in the adobe cook house, another man on the ground outside. The sergeant was a "little, humble, obedient man with a great hooked nose, large divergent ears, and wide blue eyes — simple, sincere, and unquestioning," said James Hopper. The remaining five lay on cots in the sleeping tent, next to the forage tent full of feed and bundles of wild chino grass bought from Mexican gatherers.

"The attack was made about 11:30 P.M.," said Captain Cole, "and was first discovered by the two men on guard." Legend has it that from the corral, a sentry saw armed men advancing in the dark and that he immediately blasted off every shot in his revolver to arouse his comrades. At any rate, the shooting started.

Bullets whizzed like hornets, as one sentry ran into the cook shack and the other into the forage tent. From the sleeping tent one of the men yelled to the sergeant, "Here we come!" Three men dashed to the comparative safety of the cook shack. The fourth joined the sentry in the forage tent, where they hid behind bundles of feed, cut holes in the canvas, and fired at the bandits.

In a murderous exchange at the cook house, bandits and soldiers fired in and out at each other. As Cap Wood reported soon after, the inside adobe walls showed many holes, most of the bullets having come through the door and windows. "Also," he said, "from pools of blood within twenty feet of the quarters, it was evident that the fighting was at close range." The shooting continued, Wood said, "for at least a half hour after I saw the light of the burning building."

About three in the morning, the raiders hit upon a grisly idea: Burn the *soldados* out! No common fuel burns hotter or faster than a thatch of dry, boiled-out *candelilla* weed like that on the metal roof. Bandits threw torches of kerosene-soaked rags, and up it went. If the men inside had a little water to drink, they had none to fight the fire. "The little garrison held out," said Captain Cole, "until most of them were literally roasted."

Though Compton did not say so in his testimony, the *Alpine Avalanche* said that the storekeeper "fired a hundred and fifty rounds from his house." That he did so is not likely, as he had a more immediate problem on his hands. "Before the soldiers broke for liberty out of this burning building," Compton said, "I couldn't do nothing with my little girl, nine years old.

My two boys were still asleep. She kept hollering and crying, she wanted me to take her over to the wash woman's house. I told her I would if she would hush crying and get on my back so I could carry her.

"It must be about a hundred yards over there. The wash woman told me she would take her. She wrapped her up in a black shawl, like all Mexican kids are wrapped up. Then I started back to the house to get those boys that were asleep."

But Compton was cut off, and the boys were stranded. "I got between the boiler room and the blacksmith shop," he said, "about fifty or seventy-five yards from my house. I saw when the soldiers broke for liberty."

The cook house roof roared with writhing flames as burning thatch fell on the trapped men. It seems that Sergeant Smyth directed the order of their flight.

Pvt. William Cohen, a sentry from the horse trap, climbed out through a window. "Entire top of head blown off by a shotgun blast, horribly burned," wrote Captain Cole.

Pvt. Stephen J. Coloe rushed out the door toward the corral, perhaps in a hopeless effort to catch a horse and run. Rifle bullets drilled him—"shot through the head, chest, and shoulder, body badly burned."

Pvt. Hudson Rogers, as Cap Wood learned, "with his clothes afire made an easy target when they dropped him only a hundred yards from the shack—shot through the head."

Until well into the next day, Pvt. Roscoe C. Tyree was missing. The last Sergeant Smyth saw of him, he said, "he was making for the hills."

Apparently Sergeant Smyth was the last to leave the burning shack. Thus, four made it, running barefoot, bleeding, and blistered, into the dark hills.

While Compton was huddled between the boiler room and blacksmith shop, the sergeant yelled, "Don't shoot, Compton! This is me, Sergeant Smyth!"

"I dropped down," said Compton, "but instead of him coming to me, he ran up a hill, and I didn't see him no more. The Mexicans followed him — looked to me like about twenty-five or thirty or more."

The two in the forage tent, said Captain Cole, "were the last men to leave the scene for the hills."

From their new positions above, the soldiers shot sporadically at the marauders until they rode away, shortly after daylight.

The enemy had been everywhere. "They attacked my house," said Compton, "and I warmed 'em up — shot at 'em. I backed up into that space by the boiler room. I didn't want anybody to get between me and that light, or shoot back and forth right around the other light that was back away from that fire, where the adobe was burning."

"I got out of the boiler room and hid behind a big rock, and stayed there the balance of the night. There was a trail going west out behind the boiler room, and while I was behind that rock — I judge it was two-thirty or three o'clock in the morning — these Mexicans left there, going to the river on horseback, all except twenty or thirty of 'em. They stayed and took the soldiers' horses and mine, and also Mr. Ellis's — took what they wanted of 'em."

"About seven o'clock they all went south. There was only one dead Mexican left on the ground. There were several puddles of blood around there, like you'd been killing a bunch of sheep."

There seems to be no truth in an *Avalanche* story that attributes special heroism to O. G. Compton, though his real action was heroic enough. He left his little girl with a neighbor and "made his way to the adobe hut where the soldiers fought so gallantly. There he found Private Tyree almost buried alive in the debris of the fallen roof. He rescued him and carried him on his back to the shelter of the hills." On the contrary, it seems that Compton never went to the hills.

While trapped behind the rock, Compton did not know that one of his little boys was dead.

Back before midnight, gunshots roused Cap Wood from sleep on his porch at Robber's Roost. At first he supposed the shooting to be in celebration of Cinco de Mayo.

When it persisted, however, he began to wonder. "I grabbed a rifle," he said, "and hurried to the house of a neighbor, Oscar de Montel. Together we set out on foot to investigate. High flames broke into the night, and the fighting was heavy as Oscar, a veteran of the Philippine campaign like me, and I stumbled through the whipping bushes and worrisome cactus. Half an hour later the firing ceased and the blaze died down." Six days later he said that they "wished to assist the garrison in any way possible."

After lying low for two hours, Wood and Oscar walked in among the Mexican dwellings on the southwest edge of the village. "Once we got closer," Wood said, "we decided that the garrison had driven off the attackers. We heard some Mexicans talking at times and decided that they were local laborers who worked there." But they were marauders, still milling about. "We passed through the commotion and loud talking," said Wood, and "when about a hundred yards from the soldiers' quarters, we saw horses picketed close to the road." After breaking the corral gate and scattering, they had been rounded up by the bandits.

When Wood and Oscar came within about a hundred feet of Compton's store, "a heavy silence filled the air, and we saw only one lantern — it was moving about the field near the burned adobe."

Suddenly, a bandit sentry thirty feet away, rifle pointed, exclaimed, "*Quién vivi?*"

A proper answer would have been either "Viva Villa!" or "Viva Carranza!" signifying allegiance.

Startled, Oscar blurted out, "*Quién es?*" making targets of both men.

"The sentinel emptied his gun at us as we ran through the dark, barely dodging the whizzing bullets," Wood said. "Realizing that we were in the midst of Mexican raiders and were probably surrounded, we ran east toward the hills. We heard several men moving in our direction but avoided them and reached the top of the lower hills."

Atop the same little mesa, Wood and Oscar came across two Americans. "We called them to us," Wood reported. "They were Privates Dempsey and Croskem — Dempsey in his underclothes and without shoes." In his later account, Wood said that they "were haggard and tired" and were disappointed that they had inflicted only one wound from the forage tent.

As daylight spread over the smoking ruins of Glenn Springs, Cap and Oscar looked down. "At dawn about twenty-five raiders saddled and packed their horses and those of the soldiers," Cap said, "and as the sun rose higher, they moved toward the Rio Grande."

The bandits carried off money from the post office and store, along with loads of canned food and clothing. Disgusted by sauerkraut, they had dumped the contents of those cans on the ground. They were also unwilling to pack heavy bags of flour and corn, though some feared they might come back to steal them later. "The other raiders, forty or so, had left during the night for Boquillas," according to Wood.

At about 8:30 A.M., the bandits gone, the four unharmed men came down from their mesa, now to serve as comforters. The place seemed deserted, but they soon encountered two wounded men. "Private Birck was shot through both legs, and Private Defrees was badly burned about the head and shoulders." Wood later told Hallie Stillwell that some of the survivors "had blistered as large as a man's hand all over their bodies." Wood, Oscar, and the uninjured men helped the wounded soldiers hobble into the Ellis house to lie down as comfortably as possible.

When they returned from gathering the wounded, Wood said, they found Compton's deaf-mute son and spotted Ellis "standing alone in the fighting area."

Somebody asked, "Where's Mrs. Ellis?"

"She's safe," Ellis replied. He had walked the twelve miles

back to find his car, which by good luck was undamaged, and now had it ready to drive to Marathon.

"At Compton's house," said Cap Wood, "we found the body of his small son lying a few feet from the door." According to Wood, the guilty bandit later explained that he called into the house, that there was no answer, and that he fired through the open doorway. The bullet ricocheted, killing the boy.

Compton later said, "My little boy, five years old, was shot through the heart. He was standing right in the middle of the room, right in front of the door." At the time an erroneous *Avalanche* report said the boy was "wounded in the leg, stomach, and chest, and his head battered in. The blood-stained floor of the room told a pitiful tale of the child's frantic efforts to escape his assassins." Such journalistic errors plant the seed of legend.

The handicapped lad was unharmed. "He stayed there in the house," said Compton. "They didn't bother him. He is deaf and dumb, and I am satisfied that some of these Mexicans knew it, because they knew how to get into the store." Wood, on the other hand, helped to perpetuate a tale that the deaf-mute boy wandered among the bandits during the shooting and was "spared by the superstitious Mexicans, who believed it was bad luck to harm a *loco*," or retarded person.

Sometime Saturday morning, said Wood, "the army replacements came in from Marfa, instead of on Friday as their order stated. They hastily loaded the truck with the bodies of the three dead soldiers and the wounded." The injured Sergeant Smyth, however, refused to leave.

On its way to Marathon, the truck was joined by the Ellis couple in their car and, of course, Compton and his deaf-mute son. Some hours later the soldiers were treated at the Marathon drug store. Compton joined his wife, and her mourning began as they sought to arrange for their son's burial. In Alpine the cavalry post received the dead soldiers' bodies for rail shipment to their families. The wounded were carried to the post hospital in Marfa.

About six-thirty Sunday morning, Captain Cole in Alpine got his orders from El Paso by "buzzer" (telegraph), and he joined Brewster County Sheriff Walton's automobile posse of "about twenty civilians, composed of Rangers, river guards, ranchers, and cowboys." Bristling with gun barrels, the car caravan rattled toward Marathon on the long drive to Glenn Springs. It pulled in there at 5:30 that afternoon, after an eleven-hour drive of about a hundred miles. High on the army's priority list now was constructing a telephone line from Marathon to the Rio Grande.

Saturday, the day before, was an agonized sequel to Cinco de Mayo. When the truck was about ready to move out with the dead and wounded, the little, big-eared Sergeant Smyth wrote a simple report to his commander. His letter gives a view into the mind of a dutiful American soldier. On May 6, 1916, he wrote:

> The Glenn Springs detachment was attacked last night about 11:45 by about 700 Villa men. We have 5 men left in camp, 3 are known dead and 1 missing. I have in camp Private Birck, shot 3 times and Private Defrees is pretty badly burned. Private Crock-

sem is OK, Private Dempsey is OK and I am OK, except my feet are so badly burned I cannot walk hardly. Private Cohen is dead, Private Rogers is dead, Private Cole is dead, and Tyree is missing, but I believe he is safe as I laid down and was shooting as he was making for the hills.

The Mexicans burned the shack down that we were in, it was an adobe shack but had wooden doors and windows and other wooden stuff inside. We stood them off all right until they burned down the adobe shack and then we had to make a run from it and we passed through some lead but they got three men, as I told you in the first of this letter.

Captain, I am staying instead of coming in as I want to be on the scene; also get even for killing our men. And, Captain, all the men stood the test great, not a one flinched. Please send plenty of ammunition, both rifle and pistol. Also please send shoes and clothes, as we all fought in our underclothes except the two men on guard, they had their clothes on at the time. I just got word that a force of Villa men made a raid on Boquillas. Also please send plenty of lime water and linseed oil for burns.

I am sending the three dead bodies of our men and also a little boy that was killed. Well, as the truck is ready I will stop and send in this letter. Please send out four pistols, as the men lost them, also one field belt, also plenty of bandages and other hospital supplies. All horses lost, also saddles, in fact everything but our rifles and my pistol.

That night, said Captain Wood, he and Oscar quartered in the Ellis house with the "nine new soldiers, keeping guards alerted in case the bandits returned for the remaining supplies." Obviously, Sergeant Smyth was present also.

As for Private Tyree, he must have returned to camp, but the extent of his injuries, if any, has not been reported. With no apparent foundation except rumor, the *Avalanche* said several days later, "Without food or water, Compton and Tyree spent a terrible day and night, not daring to return to Glenn Springs until on Sunday when they saw the autos of the Marathon posse." It was then, said the *Avalanche*, that Compton found the body of his dead son. Clearly, both Compton and the body had left Glenn Springs the day before.

While Glenn Springs burned that Friday night, terror was about to be inflicted at Boquillas, both in Texas and Mexico. The next morning there was to be armed robbery, store looting, and kidnapping.

8.

The Boquillas Robbery and Kidnapping

THE SATURDAY SUN was well up when Alice Hart saw a pack train crossing her ranch three miles west of Deemer's store. There she ran livestock and taught school in her house. The *Alpine Avalanche* said she spotted U.S. Cavalry horses, their backs loaded with provisions and goods, driven by Mexicans. She easily recognized the horses by their uniform color, build, and cropped broom-tails. Though she knew nothing as yet about the Glenn Springs raid, she figured from rumors that something was wrong in the Big Bend.

Rushing to the house of a Mexican neighbor, she begged to hire a team so she could drive over and warn Jesse Deemer. The neighbor refused, afraid that bandits might take his horses away from her. Upon her insistence, however, he lent her a span but would not go with her.

Hastening toward Deemer's, she met another friend, Clyde Dozier. Having heard that trouble was brewing, he had just then tried to reach Deemer, but a Mexican neighbor on the road had told him it was too late. By now Deemer had been captured or worse. The neighbor spoke only Spanish and said more that Dozier could not understand. When the Mexican drew his finger across his throat, Dozier assumed that Deemer was dead.

Alice drove back the way she had come and hid for several hours in the home of Mexican friends. After some planning, they put her in a wagon, covered her up, and carried her to McKinney Springs (near Glenn Springs). Along the wagon road, they met several bunches of mounted, armed bandits, some wearing Mrs. Ellis's hats, and one shading himself with her parasol. Before sundown Alice was lodged at McKinney Springs.

Unlike the Glenn Springs story, told in some detail by eyewitnesses, that of the Boquillas raid comes mostly second or third hand.

As for the attackers, Capt. C. W. Cole learned that the Glenn Springs–Boquillas raid was carefully planned by Villista Colonel Rodriquez Ramirez. Starting with a band of seventeen men at El Piño, Mexico, Ramirez led them across the Rio Grande about twenty-five miles upriver from Glenn Springs. While they hid in camp, he was joined by still more men. Going back into Mexico, they moved down the river, and the band grew to a frightening number—some say as many as four hundred.

On May 5 they divided into two columns. The one under Ramirez seems to have crossed at San Vicente to march across the southern Big Bend country toward Glenn Springs. The second, smaller band, led by Carranzista Lt. Col. Natividad Alvarez, remained in Mexico until they sneaked up on Deemer's store the next morning. After looting the store, the bandits waited for part of the Ramirez gang to join them with pack animals and wagons.

In Mexico near the San Vicente crossing on May 5, a tall, powerful American black, Monroe Payne, was about to become an important player in turbulent events.

Forty-four years old, he was a cowboy on the Buttrill ranch in the Rosillos Mountains of the Big Bend, and his house and family were at Bone Springs. On his fateful day, he crossed at San Vicente to see about his own thirty head of cattle grazing on the Treviño ranch.

Later that day, as Payne told his son, Marcello, he suddenly was looking down the gun barrels of Natividad Alvarez and his men. They beat him, robbed him, held him captive, and before

Saturday's sunup, forced him to guide them to Deemer's store.

Purveying an apparent rumor or tale, James Hopper wrote for *Collier's* magazine, "The bandits caught him asleep in the sand on the Mexican side, whither he had gone on an obscure goat deal." Hinting that Payne was a thief, Hopper said that such deals were common and were no cause for excitement. Even so, there is little reason to doubt Marcello's story about his father.

Son of a Fort Clark Seminole scout, Payne was born at Bracketville and reared on a Seminole land grant in Mexico. At twenty-two he returned to Texas, where he began his work on the Buttrill ranch and settled down with his family.

Independent of his Boquillas adventure, legend has made Monroe Payne something of a hired gunslinger. It is said that, while in Mexico as a youth, he was drafted into the army of Pres. Porfirio Díaz. When the revolution began, he joined with the Carranza forces, rising to the rank of colonel. Badly wounded in a skirmish at Durango against Villa's men, he supposedly was pensioned from the Mexican army and moved into the Big Bend, where he acquired a small plot to raise sheep and goats. In need of more income, he allegedly sometimes went back to Mexico to hire out himself and his gun.

About 1914, as the story goes, he was taken on for such a job by the TO ranch, which consisted of 1,256,000 acres in Mexico and spread out from seventy-five miles south of Juárez toward Ojinaga. Working closely with the TO foreman, Payne is supposed to have helped hire about thirty cowboy-*pistoleros* to round up what was left of the TO's fifty thousand steers and cross them into Texas. These cowboys could expect shoot-outs with cattle thieves almost every foot of the way. For these weeks of herding and gun work, Payne and each of the others was to be paid one thousand dollars.

Payne's quickness to defend his dignity is seen in another tale of legendary proportion. During a severe drouth in the 1920s, many Big Bend ranchers supplied themselves with water at Bone

Springs, where Payne lived. It is said that a cowboy by the name of Nay Good, called "Fatty," drove to the spring with water barrels in his wagon. His southern temper flared when the black Monroe Payne drove ahead of him to fill his own barrels, showing no deference to the white man.

Fatty screamed at him to pull back and let a white man go first. Payne responded by whipping his pistol out of his leggings pocket and whacking a bloody gash into Fatty's skull.

Fatty unhitched one of his mules and raced bareback to ranch headquarters. Here he begged his friend Graham Barnett to give him a gun so that he could kill Monroe Payne. Ignoring Fatty's plea, Barnett rode out to confront Payne himself. They met at Persimmon Gap, both on horseback.

Knowing Barnett's reputation as an incredibly fast, deadly marksman, Payne wisely said, "I was coming to apologize." Barnett laughed, and Payne joined in.

Then — so the tale goes — Barnett went up to Payne and slapped him in the face. Though set afire inside by this gross insult, Payne stifled his wrath.

Barnett said something like, "I'm going to let you clear leather with one of them guns, then I'm going to blow you up, nigger."

Payne sat like a statue — he knew he would not have a chance. Then, spurring his horse into a run, Barnett headed back to camp.

Less legendary than these yarns are events at Boquillas in 1916. It was easy pickings for the robbers as they broke into the deserted store about daylight on Saturday. When Deemer came along, said Hopper, "there were bandits all over the place lugging out his wares."

Philosophically, Deemer said, "Hello, I've been expecting you for a long time." Hopper reported that Deemer helped the bandits load his own stuff on his own wagon.

In formal accusations Deemer and Payne said that Natividad Alvarez and three other men had leveled their guns at Deemer and relieved him of thirty-six dollars in pocket money, including a twenty-dollar goldpiece. Supporting Alvarez with their guns were Macario Alvarez, Benito Atayada, and Jesus Portillo. Furthermore, Macario was accused of stealing, at rifle point, six dollars from Demitrio Garza.

In looting the store, Deemer said Mariano Atagado stole fifty sacks of flour (total value, sixty dollars). Of course, the bandits took much more.

After the bandits emptied the store and loaded the plunder, said Hopper, "The last seen of Deemer, he was smoking his pipe, perched on a pyramid of goods that he was driving in his own wagon drawn by his own horses across the Rio Grande into Mexico."

Behind Deemer's wagon plodded the enormous Monroe Payne. A news photographer described him as "a person such as

I have never seen before—but everybody in the Big Bend is like nobody I ever saw before."

In his official report, Cavalry Capt. C. W. Cole said that Deemer's store worker, Pablo Alcala, was also abducted. Apparently quickly released, Pablo vanishes from all accounts, except to be named later as a trial witness against the bandits. Not far from Deemer's, another store operated by a man named García, was not bothered.

About 10 A.M., before the robbers of Deemer's store crossed their wagons and captives into Mexico, they were joined by bandits and the pack train Alice Hart saw coming from Glenn Springs. They were about to pull their third raid in two days.

At Boquillas, Mexico, at the head of about twelve men, Alvarez surprised the mine store, sacked it, and seized eight Americans. They were mine superintendent Carl Halter, assayer R. R. Hasbrouk, mine employees W. T. Butler, Nick Postrius, N. R. McKnight, George Scott, and Anthony Swayne, and mine physician Dr. Powers, whom, according to Captain Cole, they may have brought over from Deemer's.

A few days later, intelligence was gathered by U.S. Cavalry Lieutenant William A. Raborg. Writing thirty-eight years later, he said the bandits waited in the brush for one of the truck drivers to come down from the mine to the river, where they unloaded the truck. There they surprised them. "A number of bandits climbed into the truck and hid on the floor. When all was set, they forced the driver back to the mine. There was nothing to indicate that it was not the usual empty truck returning for ore. Then the bandits jumped out, rifles in hand." As Raborg understood it, the robbers found little at the mine worth stealing.

In what seems to be the only firsthand account of the Boquillas incident, Carl Halter said to reporters in Marathon that

a dozen Mexicans came to the mine Saturday morning, bringing with them two of our truck drivers. They robbed me of my watch and sacked the houses and then ordered us into a truck, which they loaded with oil and gasoline.

The bandits, led by Colonel Natividad Alvarez, a Villista, treated us courteously, saying they were going to take us to Torreon, but would send us back in a month.

We started toward Ocampo but returned to Deemer's store to take on supplies. We then moved on to a water hole and stayed there until Sunday morning. I believe we made about eighteen miles that day, but we worked on the truck Sunday night when we went to sleep under it. [Did they sabotage the vehicle?]

A Mexican man went forward to get some mules for a wagon which had been seized. Monday morning other Mexicans went forward, leaving only three to guard us [including Alvarez].

We then determined to escape and, while the bandits were pushing on the truck, we jumped them from behind, jerked their guns from their pockets and made the Mexicans prisoners.

We then walked twelve miles across country to save distance and turned them over to the civilian posse at Boquillas.

This transfer of prisoners was made in Texas on Monday, May 8. In the 1930s Walter Prescott Webb asked a Texas Ranger in the Big Bend how they could arrest a Mexican for a crime committed in Mexico. The Ranger replied, "Well, you see, we kinda have to stick together down here. Of course it was wrong—they ought to have killed 'em." The bandits had, however, committed armed robbery at Deemer's store in Texas, and for that they were indicted and tried.

There might well have been killing in this incident, but not by the posse. Writing in 1954, retired Colonel Raborg recalled a somewhat different version of what was told to him by the mining engineer, "Mr. Holbrook [Halter]," shortly after his escape. Raborg wrote that, having looted the mine, the bandits

took the truck and the American mining personnel riding in it as passengers. The truck could not keep up with the mounted men and frequently stalled in the sand. After considerable delay in this manner, the bandits left a guard of seven men with the truck and the prisoners and rode ahead on their horses.

The next morning [Monday] the Americans arranged so as to maneuver the truck so that it became solidly stuck. Then they supervised the placing of the Mexican guard on the wheels so as to push it out. On a prearranged signal they attacked the Mexicans, four of whom were killed outright.

The remaining three were captured and brought back to Boquillas as prisoners of the mine men — the tables were reversed. The fight for the truck took place near Airises.

These captives were ringleader Natividad Alvarez, Macario Alvarez (his brother?), and Mariano Atayada. Their trials, and that of a fourth, Jesus Portillo, began four months later at Alpine.

It must be expected that tales about the Boquillas raid, kidnapping, and escape contain legendary details that are sometimes impossible to disprove or corroborate. Some say that the captive Americans only pretended that something was wrong with the truck, lying that the radiator had overheated. Thus, the guard was reduced to three when the other bandits were sent forward to fetch water. Others say that while the three remaining bandits vainly pushed on the truck, the driver kept the gear in reverse. Suddenly, they say, he shifted to neutral, the guards fell on their faces, and the captives quickly snatched the guards' weapons and gained their freedom. It has even been said that the Americans drove the truck back to Texas, forcing the prisoners to walk ahead.

A considerable variation from mine superintendent Halter's story was reported by Wally George in *True West*. George says that Dr. Homer Powers, a physician from San Angelo, was driving his Model-T Ford, returning from Terlingua, where he had treated a patient. He arrived at Deemer's store just in time to be captured by bandits. The outlaws then forced Dr. Powers to drive Deemer and Payne across to the Mexico Boquillas mine headquarters and store. "When the three miners, who recognized Dr. Powers, left their guns and the safety of the mine," said George, "the bandits charged out of hiding and surrounded them." A little later, he added, the bandits shoved the doctor's Model-T off a bluff into the river.

By this time Texas Rangers were scouring the Big Bend desert and mountains for suspected bandits. A Ranger friend told

Tony Hess of Alpine that they caught and shot several Mexicans near Glenn Springs. "They just stood 'em against a wall," Tony said, "and gave 'em the business."

In its work the posse did not just take Alvarez and his companions into custody. They wished also to seek out and intimidate collaborators with the bandits. In their operation they confronted Deemer's neighbor García, whose trading post and post office had not been touched. A tale reported by Clifford B. Casey says that lawmen collared García and gave him twenty-four hours to get himself south of the Rio Grande. Supposedly, García replied that all he needed was twenty minutes.

On Wednesday, May 10, a great dust cloud heralded the arrival at Deemer's store of the U.S. Cavalry in force. They meant business.

9.

The Cavalry Strikes Back

DOWN ON THEIR KNEES, a handful of reporters shot craps in a hall at the Hotel El Paso del Norte. When a house detective threw them out, they rented rooms elsewhere. Their job was to cover talks between U.S. Army generals and Carranzista General Álvaro Obregón on the withdrawal of American troops from Mexico. Prompted by the April raid on Columbus, New Mexico, Gen. John J. Pershing was heading a punitive expedition in a vain effort to capture Pancho Villa.

Suddenly, hell broke loose at Glenn Springs and Boquillas — three soldiers and a little boy were murdered, ten Americans held hostage. The fuse was lit to propel yet another thrust across the border.

When editors demanded coverage, the newsmen, including a newsreel cameraman, rented a couple of square, black sedans, threw in their grips, and rattled on the dirt roadway to Marathon and Boquillas. If they had not, there would have been little public information to describe the U.S. Cavalry's reprisal against Mexico after those raids. Perhaps the fullest account, though flawed, is that of James Hopper in *Collier's* magazine.

The cavalry's mission was fourfold: (1) rescue the kidnapped men — whose numbers quickly shrank to two, Jesse Deemer and Monroe Payne; (2) recover as much plunder as they could; (3)

seek out and capture known bandits; and (4) build a telephone line from Marathon to the Rio Grande.

From Fort Bliss, Troops A and B of the Eighth Cavalry were ordered to the Big Bend border. Fort Clark at Brackettville sent Troops F and H of the Fourteenth. From Fort Sam Houston came a Signal Corps group for the telephone job. Col. Frederick W. Sibley turned all operations over to the command of Maj. George T. Langhorne, a handsome, literate officer with a big Cadillac touring car as well as a couple of fine horses. Sporting a gentlemanly mustache, he was a stately rider.

The trip from El Paso to Boquillas comprised two hundred and fifty miles by rail to Marathon and after that almost a hundred saddle-miles to the Rio Grande. In El Paso on Sunday, May 8, at 4:00 P.M., horses, men, and gear clattered onto the railroad cars, with them the major's Cadillac. On Monday at 10 A.M., the train clanged and whistled into Marathon. In an hour the men were saddled, packed, and moving south down the trail. Along went the roadster, and in the dusty wake jounced the sedans of the newsmen. Two and a half days after that — on Wednesday — the troops pulled up to Deemer's deserted, ransacked, but undamaged store, reporters tagging along.

Almost immediately, 110 cavalrymen with supply wagons splashed into Mexico at San Vicente. By now the bandits had a five-day head start. In pursuit were the first American troops to cross the Rio Grande in force since the Mexican War of 1848.

Upon reaching the river, Major Langhorne ordered the reporters to stay behind in Texas. But then the one and only army supply truck balked. This truck, said Hopper, "was a delusion and a scandal. It would go pretty well at a wise old pace of about four miles an hour when there was nothing on it. But when it was loaded, it simply churned in one place, roaring and screeching like a buzz saw." The dying truck put life back into the newsmen.

When they offered to help Major Langhorne by hauling military supplies in their own cars, he consented. As "civilian packers," they drove with the backseat of each sedan crammed with four hundred pounds of equipment. The backseat of the major's Cadillac also hauled its share.

Thus accepted, said Hopper, the journalists "were considered as part of the family." At nightly campfire sessions with his officers, the major included the newsmen and gave courteous ear to their "little say as to the morrow's plans." They had not been treated so well in Pershing's foray.

Barely into Mexico, the major was handed a written proposition from the bandits. Deemer and Payne were being held at El Piño, and their captors would trade them for Lt. Col. Natividad Alvarez and the others captured by the miners. Now the two Americans were hostages in the classic sense. Believing that the bandits were only fifteen miles ahead and that they did not know the cavalry was on their trail, the major acted fast.

He quickly formed a motorized assault team. Loading his Cadillac and the sedans with two dozen of his best sharpshooters, he led the sputtering, bouncing rush to attack the enemy. Just as rapidly, he learned that the wrinkled desert and woody brush resist haste. When he found his assault unit slowed to four and a half miles per hour, he stopped the cars and waited for his horsemen to catch up from the rear. They camped, and the next morning a forced march began.

Hopper described that grueling march: "At first it was blinding white sand. Then it was half rock and sand, ribbed with sharp, corroded hills, cut by dry arroyos. No vetegation but a dust-heavy shrub here and there, or one of those strange looking long poles with a flaming flower at the top [*ocotillo*].

"What little water there was, they found in seep holes. The leading horses of the column would drink the seep hole dry, and then the others would wait around long enough till enough water seeped in once more—by which time the first would be thirsty again. When they did find a spring, it was hot—good for rheumatism, but they didn't have rheumatism."

In that severe land, they came upon only three ranches, each consisting of a single adobe hut and a few goats. Col. (then Lt.)

William A. Raborg's log said that the route went through places called Socontal, Taraises, and Los Alamos. Troops and wagons of the Eighth Cavalry went ahead, followed by those of the Fourteenth.

The soldiers were eager and resourceful, said Hopper, and "everyone was nice to everyone else." Along the way they killed a cow, and instead of feasting on the best cuts and discarding the rest, they cut the meat into strips and dried it for a hungry future. In due time they made tortillas from Deemer's flour, which they recovered from bandits.

"It was a desolate land," as Hopper described it, "hot, lonely, dusty, thirsty. But the men kept on plunging into it in terrific marches. They knew now that the bandits were not far away and that Deemer and Payne were still with them. Advices became more precise, more encouraging. They were gaining fast." But up ahead, Jesse Deemer faced death, and Monroe Payne proved himself a hero.

When the bandits had settled in camp at El Piño, some of them were determined to shoot Deemer. To prevent Payne's being a witness, they told him they had dropped a rifle some distance back and ordered him to fetch it. He consented.

After starting out, Payne grew suspicious and ran back. The captors had their guns aimed at Deemer and were uttering threats, warming themselves up to murder.

Payne rushed to Deemer's side and exclaimed, "Mister Deemer, if they gonna shoot you, they got to shoot me."

No coward himself, Deemer said, "Oh, go on, Payne. Don't be foolish. Get right out of here."

Payne insisted, "No, sir! We got caught together, and we'll stick together."

The Seminole is said to have stood so close to Deemer that it was impossible to shoot one without shooting both.

Now some of the bandits came to Deemer's aid. One wanted to spare him because he had given food to the bandit's starving wife and child. Others, who had been customers at the Boquillas store, said Deemer had befriended them and should not be harmed. Upon their pleas, he was spared.

The cavalry was closing in. At a seep hole called Sanchez, they heard that the bandits were indeed at El Piño. They saddled, mounted, and rode without a break from six in the afternoon until four the next — twenty-two hours. After resting for four hours, they were up and off again. At four the next morning, they had El Piño surrounded.

"But," said Hopper, "the bandits were not in it. They had gotten wind of the pursuit and fled."

Now about a hundred miles into Mexico, the troopers began searching every adobe and *jacal.*

In the doorway of an adobe, stood Deemer, houseguest of the village *jefe.* A moment later Monroe Payne appeared behind him. The bandits had abandoned them — the cavalry's mission was accomplished.

Reportedly Deemer's first words were, "How is the Verdun battle going?"— Germany was at war with France.

Expecting some expression of relief and gratitude, "The officers were astonished," according to Hopper.

Later that evening they were even more astonished, if not resentful. Out of courtesy, Major Langhorne invited Deemer to join him at dinner. But Deemer, said Hopper, "in his slow, large way pleaded a previous engagement — and went off to dine with Mexican friends in one of the village's lowly *jacals.*"

From that moment forward it appears that any esteem Jesse Deemer and the army may have had for each other vanished. In addition, Colonel Raborg recalled that "Deemer gave a confused and sometimes contradictory story about his capture. In part he claimed that he was acquainted with some of the bandits."

The troops had just set up camp at El Piño when a fresh report said that bandits were in nearby Rosita. The men were eager to pursue, and Major Langhorne formed a second motorized assault squad. "I dropped my coffee," said Lt. Stewart W.

Cramer, "borrowed a rifle and two bandoliers of ammunition from the soldier nearest me, and we started after them."

In his touring car, Major Langhorne led the two sedans loaded with a dozen marksmen for a surprise attack. Near Rosita they saw four or five men dash out of a house and into brush so thick that the cars could not follow. Another man leaped onto his horse and galloped away on the road.

According to Ronnie Tyler, several soldiers and the major piled into the Cadillac and roared after the man, blazing away. "The last we saw of him," said Cramer, "the big car was bounding over the ditches and bushes like a steeplechaser, to the tune of merry cannonading." The Mexican horseman eluded this attack, apparently unhurt.

But Langhorne used his open-top car as an offensive weapon again elsewhere. Bouncing across the desert, Langhorne leveled his .45 on the enemy, his sergeant-driver directing fire.

According to Hopper, "In his big touring-car Langhorne flushed a bandit band. They scattered and he went after two of them, firing as he charged, over the dashboard. He was making good practice but had not counted on the patriotism of his chauffeur. So eager became the chauffeur for the success of the pursuit that he began to help the major in his shooting by observing the result of each shot." The sergeant shouted, "a little too high," "a foot to the right," or "Jesus! You almost got him! Just an inch to the left!"

Hopper continued, "Watching where the bullets were going, he forgot to watch where the car was going. It went into an arroyo. The entire party parabaloed through the air, and there was joy all around."

If Major Langhorne put a bullet into either of his targets, Hopper did not report it.

With El Piño as a secondary base of operations, the major sent two detachments seventy-five miles farther into Mexico. Under Captain Rhea, the first detachment returned with some of the cavalry horses stolen at Glenn Springs. With this detachment also returned a story that the officers tried, said Hopper, to keep

"dark and secret." It leaked out anyhow that Captain Rhea's men had "rounded up a bunch" of Mexicans and having surrounded them, "practically annihilated" them.

The second group, apparently consisting of eight men, was led by Lieutenant Cramer, who was ordered to scout Castillón Ranch for rumored bandits and return to El Piño. Before heading out, Cramer called the major's attention to the sterility of the land and requested food from the regimental stores. His request was denied. Major Langhorne told Cramer that his assignment promised "valuable experience" and would allow him to "exercise great ingenuity." Cramer's first act of ingenuity was to have his sergeant buy what food he could from the soldiers and the people of Rosita.

Early in his march, Cramer hit the jackpot. The sun was getting low, and the men hoped to camp at the Santa Anita well. They dismounted and cautiously ascended a slope to the ridge. From there they looked down on a windmill surrounded by armed men with horses, mules, and a Mexican cart with two huge wooden wheels. They had unwittingly stumbled onto the bandits.

About an hour after sundown, the soldiers began to shoot, hitting one bandit. They stormed over the ridge and down to the windmill, dropping two more. The other bandits ran away in the dusk, apparently escaping with only their handguns.

An old man who did not flee raised his hands and explained that he was a *pacifico* (nonbelligerent) and had been captured by the bandits several days before. One of his hands was bleeding, shattered by a cavalry bullet. While in pursuit of the running bandits, Cramer left the wounded *viejo* under guard.

Having scattered the enemy, Cramer and his men returned to the well hoping for a long drink of water and a good night's rest. Their hope crumbled when they found that the guards had confined the old man in the well and that his profusely bleeding hand had made the water unfit to drink.

Cramer's tired and thirsty men rounded up what the bandits had left behind — seventeen horses and mules, nine rifles, two swords, a number of saddles, bridles, and packs, and the cart. Then they began their exhausted, dry, dark march in search of water.

The next day about sunset at a place called Cerro Blanco, a sentry of Captain Rhea's unit shouted alarm when he saw a cloud of dust coming his way. "First," said Hopper, "came two Mexican carts, each pulled by three mules of unequal size, hitched side by side." These carts with their crude rail sideboards and screeching wheels "were driven by strange, tall, bronzed beings topped by high-peaked Mexican sombreros. Behind them came more strange beings on horseback." Before them, they drove a bunch of Mexican mules and burros, mixed with a few U.S. Cavalry horses.

Just as the sentry was about to shout an alarm, off came the sombreros, and the riders tore the air with yelling—Cramer's detachment had returned to a joyful reunion.

In one of the carts lay two wounded Mexicans. One was probably the *viejo;* the other had been shot seven times—"a tribute," said a trooper, "to the marksmanship of our army." Also in the cart were several other prisoners. In the second cart, making a bed for the wounded, was much of Jesse Deemer's stolen property: overalls, jumpers, hats, denim britches, calico dresses, shoes, and even field hoes.

Colonel Raborg recalled, "Near Rancho Castillón a number of the bandits were overtaken and killed or captured before scattering into the hills. Some of the loot was recovered at this point." He added that the farthest point south reached by the troopers was Sierra Mojada.

Their mission was totally accomplished: captives rescued, stolen goods and animals recovered, alleged bandits captured or killed. Nevertheless, it was Major Langhorne's desire to march on. His desire, however, was countermanded by an order from Washington, D.C., because fifteen hundred "Yaqui soldiers" were about to attack his force. Return to Texas they did, back across that 175 miles of corrugated desert, convinced in themselves that there were no Yaquis within several hundred miles.

Hopper reported that this second punitive expedition came off without loss or sickness of either man or animal. It proved, he said, "that the American army possesses to the highest point the efficiency of its traditions and its history: the efficiency of the plains, the Far West, of Indian fighting." But he questioned whether they were ready to face " a modern and scientific army."

Soon put to the test in World War I, the army belied Hopper's misgiving.

Ronnie Tyler judged that Langhorne's "foray was in many ways more successful than General Pershing's more widely publicized pursuit of Villa, for the general returned with no such tangible symbols of conquest."

10.
Bandits on Trial —
Guardsmen on Guard
and in Print

AFTER THE BIG BEND tragedy, a few bandits were jailed, and U.S. Army and National Guard troops became a reassuring fixture in the region. Nevertheless some townships as good as strapped on their guns.

In Alpine, for example, a unit of the Home Guard was mobilized. Two weeks after the Glenn Springs–Boquillas trouble, their instructions were printed in the *Alpine Avalanche:* "In case of attack or riot, general alarm will be sounded. Night guards will remain on streets and quell any disorder. All members of Guard when answering alarm will arm themselves. In case of attack, all women and children should go to the High School Building. All members of Guard are urged to provide themselves with 150 rounds of ammunition." Under ward squad leaders Clarence Hord, W. S. Blevins, and M. S. Burke, the Home Guard also obligated itself to fighting fires.

When Sheriff Allen Walton and his posse drove back to Alpine from Boquillas, they brought four handcuffed prisoners and locked them in Brewster County's "Crossbar Hotel." To the three captured by the miners was added Jesus Portillo. The four prisoners gazed out through iron lattice until the September session of the Sixty-third District Court. For some reason, not one was charged with kidnapping.

In the grand jury indictments and the trials, however, there seems to have been a decided effort to make scapegoats of ring-leader Natividad Alvarez and perhaps his brother Macario Alvarez.

Of the six indictments against Natividad, four were on counts of murder. They declared that in Glenn Springs on May 5, 1916, he "with force of arms did unlawfully with malice aforethought kill and murder" three U.S. soldiers and four-and-a-half-year-old Oscar Garnett Compton "by then and there shooting [them] with a gun."

A puzzling fact is that Natividad seems to have been nowhere near Glenn Springs, nor were any of the officially named witnesses, with the possible exception of one listed as "Mrs. Oscar Menton"— perhaps a garbling of Montel. It was Oscar de Montel who went down from Eagle's Nest with Capt. C. D. Wood to look into the Glenn Springs turmoil. There is no reason to believe that his wife went with them, much less that she saw Natividad shoot anybody. Her name no longer appears in Brewster County records of these events. Whatever evidence the witnesses had must have been circumstantial only.

When the trials of Natividad for these alleged killings came to the bench, that for the murder of the Compton boy was conducted first. As an impartial jury could not be mustered in Brewster County, venue was changed to Jeff Davis County. Promptly, Natividad was hauled away and penned in that county's "Bat Cave." In January, 1917, this murder charge was "dismissed on motion of the District Attorney," apparently because of lack of evidence. Natividad went back to jail in Alpine, and in February charges against him for killing the soldiers also were dropped. Before this time, however, he already had fallen under heavy sentence.

In Alpine back in September, Natividad seems to have invited the boom to fall on himself. He supposedly preferred to sit out the Mexican Revolution in the Texas State Penitentiary rather than go back to Mexico as a failure to confront his Carranzista superiors. They could be merciless.

The effective indictment against Natividad said that he held a rifle on Jesse Deemer, putting him "in fear of life and bodily injury," thereby compelling him to hand over his twenty-dollar gold piece, a ten-dollar bill, and a dollar in change. Whether Natividad split the take with the three sidekicks accused of simultaneously holding rifles on Deemer is unknown. Aside from Deemer, subpoenaed witnesses were Monroe Payne, Pablo Alcala (reported earlier as kidnapped), Jesus Alcala, and Demetrio Garza.

In district court, Natividad pleaded guilty of this offense, and he "persisted in entering such a plea" when Judge Joseph Jones "admonished him of the consequences." The judge then addressed the jury: "You are instructed to find the defendant guilty as charged in the indictment, and so say you in your verdict, assessing his punishment at death or confinement in the penitentiary for any term of years not less than five." Promptly the jury returned to the box with near maximum punishment. Foreman W. A. Weakley announced, "We the jury find the defendant guilty and assess his punishment at ninety-nine years in the penitentiary."

In the one remaining indictment against him, Natividad was said to have robbed Demetrio Garza at rifle point on that same night of May 5. Demetrio surrendered to him a five-dollar bill and about a dollar in coin. Though Demetrio heads the list of witnesses in the indictment, his name is not among those of the witnesses subpoenaed for the trial. The other witnesses called to appear before the grand jury and district court are the familiar four: Deemer, Payne, and the two Alcalas. Judge Jones dismissed this charge against Natividad Alvarez. Again, why?

He also threw out those against Marcario Alvarez, Benito Ayada, and Jesus Portillo for abetting Natividad in relieving Deemer of his pocket money. After four months in jail, Benito and Jesus probably were released to the U.S. Immigration Service for deportation to Mexico.

Marcario, however, stayed behind bars, as the court had ordered that another case against him be "continued." He was accused of holding up Demetrio Garza with a gun and taking from him "one five-dollar bill" and "one dollar in silver coin." The usual four, plus Demetrio Garza, were subpoenaed.

The case was continued with change of venue to Terrell County. With a year of jail now behind him, Marcario appeared with another man in a consolidated trial before district court in Sanderson on June 8, 1917. Jury foreman James Kerr reported, "We the Jury find each if the defendants Guilty and Essess their punishment at 5 years in the State Penitentiary."

Marcario, as Natividad before him, was "remanded to jail" until the sheriff could "obey the directions of this sentence" by transferring him to an official of the Texas State Penitentiary.

Thus the legal machinery ground out judgments on the four men captured in connection with the Glenn Springs–Boquillas raid, two of them bound for "The Walls" at Huntsville. Justice seems to have completed its mission — or had it?

At this point Natividad Alvarez and Marcario Alvarez disappear from public records. Neither Brewster County nor Terrell County had any evidence that these men were transferred to Texas penal authorities. Sheriff's department and jail records for those years are nonexistent — perhaps none was made in that era. A check of the state's penal records by Jim Killough did not indicate "anyone by the above names as ever being an inmate in the Department of Corrections." It is not impossible that both men were freed from the county jails on grounds of "false arrest," upon intervention of a Mexican consul. Though charged only with crimes committed in Texas they were captured by American civilians in Mexico and forced across the border and into the hands of Texas lawmen.

After the bandit trials, what became of Jesse Deemer and Monroe Payne? Deemer seems to have sold his interest in the store to his partner, Louis Ritchie of Marathon, moving then to California never to return. According to Marcello Payne, Deemer and Payne jointly sued the Mexican government for $50,565 in damages. Whether they ever collected a *centavo* is unknown.

During the trials Monroe Payne's address was the Buttrill

ranch, but soon after, according to his son Marcello, he moved his family to Marathon, where he worked as a teamster-hauler. Legends speculate on how Monroe may have died. One tale says that he was killed in a saloon fight in either El Paso or some small border town. Yet another says that he died in his sleep, laughing. Brewster County records, however, state that he died of a heart attack at home in Marathon on June 11, 1952, and was buried in one of the town's cemeteries. His usual occupation was recorded as "ranch hand."

About the time Marcario Alvarez was sentenced, Texas National Guardsmen arrived in the Big Bend to augment the U.S. Cavalry. On May 9, 1916, four days after the Glenn Springs–Boquillas raids, President Wilson ordered the guards of Texas, New Mexico, and Arizona to active duty. Texas units seem to have been placed in the Big Bend within the month. Nationally, more than a hundred thousand guardsmen were wrenched from their jobs and families and gathered at staging areas in Brownsville, San Antonio, and El Paso, Texas, and at Nogales, Arizona. By the Fourth of July, the hills of Mexico were in plain sight of disgruntled guardsmen from fourteen states. Many, if not most, of these men had joined up for the clublike companionship of their units and to pick up a little extra cash for doing little or nothing. Their present mission was to establish a military presence that would make foreign marauders think twice before putting off their dirty work in Texas or anywhere else along the border. It worked.

Down in the Big Bend country camped guardsmen from Pennsylvania as well as Texas including infantry Company I from Mineral Wells, a resort town famed for its wholesome Crazy Water and the elegant Crazy Hotel.

That is why bespectacled, thirty-one-year-old pharmacist Jodie P. Harris (perhaps Sergeant) found himself soldiering in the Big Bend, far away from the ice-cream sodas of the drugstore where he filled prescriptions. At the end of November, 1916, he said he had been in the Big Bend for six months.

Not long after his arrival, hometown bulletin boards sprouted with Harris's hand-cartooned postcards, drawn "between hikes," as he said. One pictures the Company I baseball team in action — La Noria versus Stillwell Crossing — the catcher using a meal sack for a mitt. Another shows his grueling hike along the rim of Boquillas Canyon — Strawhouse Trail — from Boquillas to Stillwell.

Remarkably, Harris produced two numbers of a hand-lettered and cartooned unofficial, tabloid-sized camp newspaper, a forerunner of *The Stars and Stripes* and *Yank*. They circulated among soldiers camped at Lanoria, Boquillas, Camp Mercer (Stillwell Crossing), Glenn Springs, Lajitas, and Terlingua. Neither the cartoons nor the text was always reverent. They often bore out an observation by Ronnie Tyler that the uprooted guardsmen "learned to hate the soldier's typical duty. They drilled, practiced marksmanship, and established camps and lines of communication. Troops on guard, troops at leisure. But no troops in battle." Prone to rumor, they "concluded that they had been called to active duty to enhance the wealth of border merchants or to fulfill the terms of some shadowy, international intrigue." Moreover, according to Jodie, they dug meaningless trenches in the roasting sun, then froze in the sleepless desert nights.

Paradoxically, some of the men including Jodie, were enchanted by the beauty of the place and were among the first to urge its being made into a national park, which of course it later was.

Jodie's first paper, *Lanoria*, vol. I, no. 1, was dated October 15, 1916, and published at Lanoria, Texas. To letter and draw his paper, Jodie sat on an ammunition box and used a soapbox for a desk. The only tools he had were pen, paper, and diluted ink — no dictionary or copyreader — and he was not much of a speller or grammarian, as his papers show. After doing four tabloid sheets, he mailed them to the *Fort Worth Press*, where engravings were made. The blocks came back to Marathon to be printed at an erstwhile newspaper plant and then somehow circulated among the forlorn guardsmen in scattered Big Bend camps. As Jodie wrote, the papers were "smuggled into the soldiers mail bag 90 miles from a post office as first class stuff."

Harris despised war. But the front page of *Lanoria* was scarcely the place for him to copy "Peace" by Dr. Frank Crane. In part it reads, "Peace means the higher manliness of the gentleman and not the cheaper manliness of the bully. . . . Peace is the ally of wisdom, generous patience, human consideration, and war is the ally of egotism, anger, cruelty, and vain glory. . . . Peace is the unshakable courage of sanity. War is the red blind courage of madness." Such words hardly bolster a soldier expected to risk his life for his country.

Moreover, in his page three editorial, he pretended to cast about for a subject. He wrote:

> Shall we begin at home with a little muck-raking? No! We have not the space to tell of the Glenn Springs raid or the Boquillas robbery led by an unscrupulous American ? grafter, maybe he is German.
> It makes us heavy hearted to think of it, for this is why we are here.
> This is why some of our best men are spending the best part of their lives 80 miles from a post office in the sand hills of the Big Bend country for a useless cause, German?
> Are we crazed with patriotism?
> Why don't we investigate?
> Will it be treason for an humble guardsman to ask, What is it all about?

On the same page Jodie penned two quips. One reads, "Thomas Jefferson says 'equal and exact rights to all men.' What are we going to do with Deemer?" The other says, "The baked beans follow the flag, and the German follows the border."

In his column headed "The Market," Jodie struck yet another jab at his scapegoat. "The smuggling of ammunition across the border to the Mexican bandits," he wrote, "is all imaginary and has been since Deemer left the country."

That was not all. In a whimsical "news" item, Jodie wrote that Guardsman Sparks (also camp barber), while out hunting for deer, got to thinking "of the natural fortification that this worthless and unpopulated country was making and how foolish the War Department was in sending the cream of the nation to this God-forsaken desert."

In his second paper, referring to Deemer and his store, Jodie remarked, "Where his custermers came from is somewhat of a mystery as no one lived there except two Mexicans. Consequently his enterprise was looked on with suspicion by all good citizens of Brewster County." He reported that Deemer claimed the bandits robbed him of eight thousand dollars in merchandise and fourteen hundred dollars in cash. When "Mr. Deemer set up a howl for troops, one troop of cavalry and a company of militia was sent to protect his property." Soon, however, "He complained to the government that the soldiers were damaging his property and asked that they be removed as they made him nervous." (Col. William A. Raborg reported that Deemer, upon his release and return from Mexico, "put in a claim for ten thousand dollars against the U.S. government for damage to willow trees on his property along the Rio Grande at Boquillas, claiming they were destroyed by the cavalry horses." Because the horses had been tied on picket lines and because an inspection found no damage, said Raborg, "It was recommended that the claim not be paid.")

Concluding, Jodie said, "He is now enjoying the comforts of sunny California, while the Texas militia is left to guard the uninhabited Big Bend — Deemer is gone — Boquillas is for rent."

In 1989 a former U.S. Air Force captain read Jodie's newspapers and concluded, "I would have him court-martialed for sedition." It seems that Jodie was indeed required to stand at attention before Captain Biggers and reply, "Yes, sir," when reminded that the Articles of War demand that a soldier may utter nothing in public print.

In consequence Jodie framed a motto for his next paper, *The Big Bend*, vol. I, no. 1, November 30, 1916. It reads, "A paper with a muzzle: Without a mission." At that time it was feared that the European war would escalate into world war, and gramophones nationwide blared a top song-hit, "I Didn't Raise My Boy to Be a Soldier." Whatever occurred at Captain Biggers's desk, *The Big Bend* was the last of Jodie's camp newspapers.

The Big Bend included much more camp news than *Lanoria* — items that throw some light on the National Guardsman's life in the Big Bend. If their daily existence was boring, their mission was fulfilled: no shooting, no problem.

In neither publication did Jodie's editorial spleen overwhelm his light treatment of what news he had to report. In *Lanoria* little news is to be found partly because, as Jodie wrote, "We had planned to get Jack Harris, the newspaperman at Stillwell, to help us with this issue. But he failed us, and we have made a mess of it — Next issue we promise to do better." Jack had "refused to have anything to do with this issue." Wise Jack. This would be John O. Harris, Jodie's brother, also of Company I.

Perhaps the most newsworthy item in the first issue tells of the "dedication" of the Company I library, consisting of five books donated by the Misses Clark of Marathon. "The company made Jodie Harris librarian," and he outlined the rules for borrowing the books and keeping them clean.

Harris reported that Captain Biggers, with Sergeant O'Dell and two recruits, hiked the payroll to Stillwell Crossing. "It taken lots of nerve and mule strength to make that trip." From Stillwell, reluctant Jack did report, "Captain Biggers brought the payroll. All of our boys have money now."

At Lanoria he reported, "We have a real doctor in our midst. He has a small size trunk full of cures." Over at Stillwell, said Jack, "The health of our camp is good — thank the Lord, for it is 84 miles to the nearest doctor."

Back at Lanoria, "The shrewd young gamblers, Gulley and Chamberlain, are teaching the young recruits how to play cards and how to roll dice. Any man can make a soldier's life pay if he knows how."

At Stilwell, "a new telephone line is quite a help in making our boys feel like they are still in a civilized country but it seems strange not to hear a woman operator on the line."—"Fishing is fine on the Rio Grande. Bill Ab has all his hooks out. . . . We get our mail once a week now. . . . All is quiet on the Rio Grande."

Above an important story, Jodie's cartoon depicts a hard-tired, back-wheel chain-drive truck with a fabric top and side curtains. Lettered on its side are the words, "TRAVELING ARMY—Y.M.C.A.—BIG BEND DISTRICT." The story reads, "Last week the traveling army Y.M.C.A. visited Stilwell and spent two days giving a motion picture each night! A phonograph was part of the entertainment, which the boys played contineously [sic] throughout the two days. This detachment is indebted to them for two of the most pleasant days spent on the border."

With cold December around the corner, the item most important to a soldier told how Uncle Sam refused to issue more blankets. A soldier is taught, said Jodie, always to "get under cover" while in action. As cold winds blew, "remembering the advice or our commanding officers, we appealed to the quartermaster for more blankets." The men were told that the Quartermaster Department was "waiting the outcome of the Mexico mediation before issuing more blankets." Many of the men wrote home for quilts, and "until they arrive we are using gunny sacks, old clothes or anything to keep WARM."

Items from Camp Mercer: "Sgts. O'Dell and Harris have floored their tents with gravel. . . . Elmo Smith is on furlough. . . . Corp. Blatherwick is confined to his cot this week, his illness being due to overeating. We had bisquits. . . . Private Schlessier and Wells bought a pint of *mescal* from a Mexican. The Doc says they will recover. . . . McMahon, a teamster who was detached from the Greenville Company to Co. I went over the hill."

Jodie recorded that at Terlingua, "One troop of the Sixth Cavelry and one company of Texas militia is stationed here. . . . As yet this paper has been unable to secure a correspondent from there."

No news from Glenn Springs except that "A and B Troops

of the 6th Cavalry are stationed there." One of Jodie's postcards depicts Glenn Springs with a "6th cavalry" camp and a "Pa. camp."

In "Sporting News" the score between the *Stilwell* River Rats and the Lanoria Well Digger Warriors was twenty-one to nine, but Jodie forgot to say who won the game or where it was played. "Todays game," however, "was called in order TO finish THE trenches before the Col. arrived." He also reported that a twenty-pound mud cat was caught. He continued, "Wong Roberts who in civil life was Mr. Roy Roberts the affable clerk at the Crazy Hotel introduced the old army game last pay day." The latter item bears Jodie's drawing of a pair of dice.

If Jodie tried to tone down his abrasive editorializing in the second paper, *The Big Bend,* he succeeded only in allowing it less space. He gave considerably more attention to feature stories and camp news.

Of the three front-page features, one praised the United States as a liberator of the oppressed, giving Cuba as an example. Another saw conditions in Mexico as deplorable and suggested that the United States give her a brotherly hand. The third was a nostalgic treatment of Thanksgiving.

In his page-two editorial, Jodie chafed behind his muzzle. He wrote, "The United States is the land of the free, the Constitution provides for free speech, but in the Articles of War appear these words, 'No officer or enlisted man will be permitted to correspond to any paper, magazine, or periodical.' An enlisted man's opinion is considered worse than worthless, and he is committing a crime a-kin to treason when he even thinks at all." Some of this must have been what his captain made clear to him.

Getting back to one of his most consistent opinions, Jodie said, "Believing that the border situation is vastly exaggerated, we the boys of Co. I have voiced our opinion, which may or may not be correct." In an adjacent item, he said, "Why a handful of the Texas National Guard is kept here no one seems to know or care. The place is as peaseful as Weatherford on Sunday, and though it may be unpatriotic we are sometimes constrained to cry out, 'How long, O Lord, how long?'"

In addition to the news bits, a few feature articles temper the fretful commentary in Jodie's papers. Usually they describe Big Bend people and their ways.

In Jodie's first paper, one of these is headed by a good-natured cartoon depicting a Hernandez couple of Lanoria, their seven children, dog, and cat, as "the only family living in our city." Hernandez and his dog, said Jodie, "herd about 50 of his goats on school-land that the government can't sell." A news item reported that the Hernandez henhouse had burned down.

The second number carries more feature material than the first. In the longest feature, which describes the Roberts *candelilla* wax plant at Stilwell Crossing, Jodie's venom leaked in. "The wax plant is a large one," Jodie said, "the total amount invested being about $500 or about as important as a sorghum mill of East Texas. Yet the owners asked for protection from the government and claimed to have had fifteen hundred dollars invested." Jodie complained, "Without investigation 30 men of Company 'I' were sent here to protect a 'squatters' property 90 miles from a rail road so situated that, in the event of hostilities, it would be 48 hours before reinforcements could arrive."

Then Jodie described the wax workers' condition. Weed gatherers were paid "$1.75 per ton in merchandise," and the owners "operate a small commessary and the laboring *peons* are charged a double price for food stuffs."

In his piece on Terlingua, Jodie pointed out that the Chisos mines "furnish about one fourth of the world's supply of quicksilver and furnishes employment for several hundred Mexicans." Also, "very little is known of the Terlingua mines as no one is allowed to enter them, and the owners are not seeking publicity."

Again Jodie spoke of the workers' situation: "Several years ago a law was passed in Texas prohibiting mill owners from using the paste-board check system in payment for labor, but evidently this law is not recognized at the Chisos mines, as the *peon* in exchange for his labor gets little more than food and clothing for himself and family."

Just when Jodie Harris was transferred out of the Big Bend is not clear. Five months after his second paper appeared, the United States entered the Great War, and Jodie served in France with the ambulance corps, either earning or retaining the rank of sergeant. Later abandoning pharmacy, he became associated with an oil company in Albany, Texas, and during World War II — ironically — he worked for the federal Office of Censorship in El Paso. Interviewed in 1953, he recalled "with mellow sentiment how the Big Bend country grew on the minds of the border troopers." In 1944 he was honored in the dedication ceremony of the Big Bend National Park as one of its earliest advocates. He died in 1960 at age 84 in the Veterans Hospital at Big Spring, Texas.

As a result of the raids on Glenn Springs and on Boquillas, both in Texas and Mexico, the U.S. Cavalry exerted its force with the second Punitive Expedition of 1916. The cavalry rescued two hostages and recovered much stolen property, including horses. American workers at the Puerto Rico mine delivered at least three prisoners to Texas lawmen, and four bandits were brought to justice. Largely because of the prompt activation of Texas and other states' National Guardsmen, Brewster County was relieved of marauders from troubled Mexico. To the west, however, despite military presence, Presidio County would be struck in 1918 by deadly raids on the Brite and Nevill ranches.

A serendipitous byproduct of the raids was the folk art of Jodie Harris. His lively, outspoken newspapers, cartoons, and postcards give the world a personally felt experience, not only of soldier life, but also of people, places, and scenery in the Big Bend of 1916.

PART IV
An Ancient Tablet — A Rugged Faith

11.

The Big Bend Tablet

WHO GETS THE distinction of being the first visitors to Big Bend National Park? There is reason to believe that they wandered in from southern Europe almost seventeen hundred years ago — or did they? But the real prize goes to an ordinary group of four family members on an outing, one of whom stumbled onto what those presumed earlier travelers left behind. It has come to be known as the Big Bend tablet.

Their adventure began at Christmastime, 1961, in San Marcos, Texas. Donald and Reva Uzzell (pronounced "You-zell") had company. Donald's mother Bernice Nickles and her husband Charles had come for a visit from Salmon, Alaska, where Charles was a bush-pilot.

When he was interviewed in 1990, Donald said, "I'm not really sure who suggested going to the Big Bend. None of us had ever been there before, and with Mother just coming out of Alaska, it seemed like a warm place to go for a vacation." They stayed in the basin and the next morning, drove out to tour the park, heading toward Boquillas Canyon. During that outing, the path of these four tourists merged with the path of ancient history.

"We didn't stop at the headquarters for any directions or information," Donald said. "We had a map — I think we got it from the room where we stayed — of some of the roads in the park." With Donald at the wheel, they were driving east on the then unpaved road when Donald turned off on a side road to the south. "To the best of my knowledge," Donald recalled "this road wasn't on the map. Anyway, I just headed off down this road, and to our surprise, we ended up at Hot Springs."

Reva and the Nickles couple poked around the abandoned trading post and tourist camp, then chose to walk up adjacent Tornillo Creek, Donald said, "looking for unusual rocks or whatever. I didn't see anything interesting about walking around and kicking up dirt, so I just sat in the car and listened to the radio."

He continued, "Now this is something that almost never happens to me: I had this sudden feeling that I wanted to get out. I just decided to climb up onto that ledge on the other side of the creek. I didn't want to wade the creek, but I did—there was very little water in it.

"Then I started climbing. Now, I'm not a cliff climber. I don't care nothing about climbing cliffs. But I started up the only place I could see that anybody could get up. I just had this overwhelming feeling that made me do this. I never can explain it.

"As I began my climb, I can remember my mother calling for me to get down before I fell. The shale was giving way under my feet at times, but that only led my determination to climb higher. The cliff was more of a challenge than a walk up a dry creek bed. I was enjoying my vacation my way."

Suddenly, when he was standing on the ledge he had set out for, it happened. "I accidentally put my hand on this opening in the cliff," Donald said, "and I could see pieces of something stacked in there. I hollered, 'Hey! There's a hole here with something in it!'" The others gathered below him.

"The hole was L-shaped," said Donald, "and the pieces all were stacked in the leg facing me. They were stacked in a row of three or four pieces to a stack. I've always wondered why there was nothing in the leg around the corner. There'd been lots of holes in this cliff, but none so perfect and none of the others had anything in them."

What Donald had found was a rectangular niche with an opening four inches wide and nine inches high that led into a little tunnel nineteen inches deep. That leg of the L contained the pieces and ran parallel to Tornillo Creek. Then the tunnel, making an abrupt right turn, extended twenty-two inches, its opening visible from the creek. The inside dimensions are constant from one end to the other. "The sides and top and floor of the hole were real smooth," said Donald. The refinement of the niche was also noted by Fort Worth writer Bernice McGee, when she inspected and measured it in 1970. She reported that "inside, the whitish walls were smooth and even, as are the ceiling and floor — so perfectly squared off inside that a mason's chisel couldn't have made an improvement."

After making his find, said Donald, "I told the others what was in the hole and, after looking at the first piece, that's when I started taking them out. Then we decided on how to get them down without damaging any of the pieces."

Despite her previous anxiety about her son, Bernice climbed up to a ledge just below him, scattering loose shale behind her. Donald's wife took a stand below her, and Charles a place yet farther down, but still rather high from the creek bed. One by one they passed the fragments to each other. Each time Charles received a piece, he descended to the flat surface, laid it on the ground, and climbed up for another — eleven trips in all.

When they came down from the bluff, they inspected Donald's find. They were amazed that the pieces fit together like a jigsaw puzzle to form an oblong, claylike tablet about twenty-one inches tall and fourteen across at its widest point. On it were clearly scratched lines of what appeared to be writing in a bizarre alphabet.

An avid photographer, Charles Nickles took several color slide pictures, which soon would be the only tangible evidence that there ever was a Big Bend tablet.

"The pieces felt real hard to me," Donald said, "and I wondered then how the pieces nearest the opening could look so weathered. You can probably tell by looking at the picture which three or four were stacked near the opening. They didn't fit together real close like the others did.

"The pieces were slick on top where the writing was and felt rough on the underside. The other sides (edges) looked like dried clay that had been broken apart. The surface where the letters were glistened like fresh-made fudge candy, and was very, very, very hard. The color was light, sort of between tan and brown.

"So after looking at it for a while, we put it in a cardboard box and took it to the park headquarters, because when we entered the Big Bend, we saw a sign that said any artifacts found in the park belonged to the park. We knew it didn't belong to us and felt that it must have great importance to the history of the park."

But the rule-abiding tourists were in for a letdown. "When we took the tablet to the headquarters," Donald said, "the man behind the counter looked rather sceptical at all of us." This man behind the counter was David Evan, who was then the park's head naturalist. Donald went on: "I think he actually thought we had just made it and brought it in as a joke. He acted like he couldn't have cared less about those pieces and asked if we didn't want to keep it for ourselves. When we refused, he took it from us reluctantly and put it under the counter.

"We gave him our names and addresses so *if* anything was found out about it, we could help out."

Confident that the fragments would be protected and studied, the tourists nosed around the park and then went home. A few months later, a letter came from the naturalist, saying that the man who had inspected the tablet could not make heads or tails of it.

Not long after Donald's find, the Nickles couple came across writings of Lewis R. Church about evidence of the presence of pre-Columbian Europeans in America. They wrote an inquiry to Church and included photographs of the tablet. Church, in turn, conferred with a Dr. Phillips, a classical languages scholar at Brigham Young University in Provo, Utah. Both men agreed that a few of the characters on the tablet resembled some letters in an ancient Greek alphabet. Otherwise, they were stumped.

In 1964, having moved back from Alaska to their native Texas, the Nickleses resumed their investigation of the clay tablets. They sought out writers with an interest in the Southwest. J. Frank Dobie's health prevented him from taking an active interest in the investigation. Five years after that, it seemed to them that a pair of Fort Worth free-lance writers might be helpful in the pursuit of its significance.

The Nickleses read an article by Bernice and Jack McGee on pre-Columbian, Scandinavian "Runestones and Tombstones" found in Oklahoma (*True West*, Winter, 1969). The authors invited anyone who knew of any strange inscriptions to respond, and the Nickles couple did, offering to send pictures. The McGees were amateur newcomers to epigraphy, the study and deciphering of ancient inscriptions. They jumped at the challenge, and subsequently gave years to unraveling the mystery of the Big Bend tablet.

It should be more widely known that there is a mass of concrete evidence suggesting the more or less random presence, even long before Christ, of maritime trading and mining Europeans, North Africans, Middle Easterners, and Asians in the West. Though the pre-Columbian voyage of Leif Ericson is recognized, it appears that there may have been other Norsemen before him, but also visitors representing the ethnic and language groups already named, including Phoenicians and Jews. They left their marks.

That all this is not generally known perhaps arises from two primary reasons. First, only since about 1950 has the study of epigraphy come to be organized. Second, those pre-Columbian expeditions had no noticeable effect on the course of the world's history. Conversely, the discovery by Columbus dramatically changed civilizations worldwide.

The pre-Columbian visitors, however, have their champions who pursue, interpret, and catalog hard evidence of those early presences among the American Indians. Perhaps the best known of these is Dr. Barraclough "Barry" Fell, whose book, *America, B.C.* (1976), presents evidence of early Europeans and others in

America well before 1492. Dr. Fell had retired from the Harvard faculty as professor emeritus of marine biology.

In *Saga America* (1980), he presents a map of the United States to identify areas where examples of non-Amerindian expressions and artifacts have been found, either etched on stone or exhumed in archeological digs. From northern California and Nevada southward to Mexico have been discovered inscriptions identified as Kufic Arabic and Libyan. From southern California across the Southwest to the Big Bend country of Texas are epigraphs in Libyan and Numibian Arabic. Many such signs in other ancient languages have been recognized east of the Mississippi and in Canada.

Excited by the opportunity to work with what Donald Uzzell had found, Bernice and Jack McGee plunged into their search for answers to vital questions. First of all, did the tablet still exist? To find out, she wrote to the Big Bend National Park, where her inquiry was referred to its chief naturalist, Roland "Ro" Wauer. He was cooperative.

In time Ro replied that he had contacted David Evan, who had misgivingly accepted the object for the U.S. government. Now stationed at Lake Head, Nevada, the naturalist remembered the artifact as a cake of sun-dried mud that could be peeled from the bottom of many a mud-soaked flat along Tornillo Creek. Also, he said, as the fragments were not weather worn, he judged it to be recently made, perhaps by these very tourists, a couple of days before. Now, however, he admitted that he might have been wrong.

To explain the disappointing fate of the tablet itself, he said that

> it lay on a window sill in my office in the maintenance building for many weeks. I showed it to any and all who might be able to shed some light on it. Everyone agreed that it had no historical significance. It disintegrated from handling, and the move down to the new administration at Panther Junction turned it into a pile of dust.

Anyway, as long as we were able to hold it together, no one who saw it believed it had any antiquity.

The most shocking opinion: "The concensus was that a Mexican goatherder had sat and doodled in the mud with a stick." None of the judgments accounted for its having been found in pieces stored in an invisible nook high on a bluff.

Evan's testimony left the finely detailed photograph by Charles Nickles as the only visual evidence that the tablet ever existed. Now to the McGees' second question: Did the little L-shaped alcove, as Donald described it, exist? The McGees would soon find out.

Before completing plans to search for the tablet's hiding place, Bernice McGee had made inquiries about the strange inscription. With his unusual name, Dr. Cyclone Covey, professor of ancient history at Wake Forest University in North Carolina, responded. He believed that the writing consisted of primitive Greek characters mixed with those of another alphabet, which neither he nor his colleagues could identify.

Respectful of Bernice's self-acquired knowledge of epigraphical studies, Dr. Covey inquired, "Have you considered that the Big Bend tablet might represent the terminal phase of an expedition that floated *down* the Rio Grande from Los Lunas, New Mexico, instead of *up?*" Many epigraphical studies had thought of early non-American visitors as reaching the West by traveling up tributaries of the Mississippi, such as the Missouri and the Cimarron. The doctor raised a new question: Could they have crossed the Pacific, not the Atlantic, to reach North America? Studies by Dr. Fell and others indicate that they certainly could have done so.

This hypothesis, said Bernice, could account for the ancient Greek tombstone identified near Cripple Creek, Colorado, a few miles north of the Rio Grande headwaters. To the south, near Albuquerque, New Mexico, near the junction of the Puerco with the Rio Grande, was the Los Lunas inscription on a cave wall, which was interpreted in 1946. Its script is early Phoenician or Hebrew (much akin), and its text is a modified version of the Ten Commandments.

These professors were going in the right direction, but their combined knowledge was not enough to interpret the Big Bend Tablet or explain its presence at Hot Springs.

In October, 1970, Bernice and Jack McGee arranged a meeting in the Big Bend with the Uzzells (now of Bastrop) and the Nickleses (of Brenham). They sought to rediscover the cramped, L-shaped niche in which Donald found the fragments. Camped at Rio Grande Village, they were joined by Ro Wauer and headed for Hot Springs.

"I don't remember that cliff being so high," Donald said. When he had made his first crumbling ascent, he was nine years younger and a few pounds lighter. For a time he paced up and down the creek bed, peering upward to study the cliff. When he felt that he had spotted his target, he climbed to the first ledge. Then he changed his mind and came down.

As he moved down the creek toward the Rio Grande, still eyeing the bluff, the party was joined by Miriam Lowrance of Sul Ross State University, where she was a professor of art. For several months Bernice McGee had exchanged letters with this dedicated collector of Indian rock art of the Big Bend. With Miriam was Wayne Weimer of Marfa, another rock art enthusiast.

By this time Ro Wauer, Charles Nickles, and Jack McGee also were climbing above the creek bed, examining the bluff. After about an hour, Donald called out triumphantly, "Here it is!"

He was amazed that it was about thirty feet above the creek and not fifteen, as he had remembered. There could be no mistake—this was it. He removed what debris there was and put it in a box, but this debris told them nothing.

Now it was Bernice McGee's turn. With her husband, Jack, as a ladder, she scrambled up with notebook and measuring tape. She recorded the little tunnel's dimensions and judged, "The four-by-nine inch opening would have protected the pieces from the wind, sun, and rain." Such protection, she believed, would account for Evan's observation that the tablet "was not weathered at all."

Without success Donald and Ro felt about in other crannies for artifacts or evidence to support their cause, finally giving up and joining the others. Then Miriam led the group to a rock etching that seemed out of character with the usual Indian work. It is reproduced in the McGees' *True West* article (July–August, 1972). This petroglyph contains strange symbols, letters, or numerals. One of these resembled a double-backed axe and was of special interest to Bernice McGee. She would learn later of its possible significance to the Big Bend tablet.

During the next couple of days, these studious tourists looked for samples of a local mud or clay that might harden into slabs that would, if well protected, hold together indefinitely. They thought they found it — a Tornillo Creek mud called "bentonite," a reddish, mineral clay with iron content, formed by decomposed volcanic ash. (It is named after Fort Benton, Montana.) The stuff absorbs large amounts of water, expanding beyond its regular size. The first builder at Hot Springs, J. O. Langford, used it as a sealant for his cane rooftops, and it is used today by ranchers to seal the bottoms of dirt water-holding tanks.

About three months later, Dr. Covey reported on the sample the McGees sent him. He said that as the material dried, it became lighter in color, approximating that in the color slide by Charles Nickles.

The 1970 expedition achieved what it set out to do. It substantiated the precise place of Donald's discovery and the setting up by Ro Wauer of a permanent Big Bend Tablet file in the park headquarters at Panther Junction. In the following year Bernice and Jack McGee gave the artifact its name in their *True West* article, "The Mystery of the Big Bend Tablet." Still nagging, however, was that the origin of the inscription and its meaning were still unknown. Having come to a blank wall, Bernice and Jack devoted their research and writing to more typical western subjects. But haunting the back of their minds for seven more years was the Big Bend Tablet. What did it say?

Their wait ended suddenly. Miriam Lowrance pointed the way, with an assist from *Readers Digest*. In its February, 1977 issue, she read a condensation of Barry Fell's book, *America B.C.*, and studied its illustrations of pre-Christian American epigraphs by Celts, Iberians, Libyans, and Norsemen. Thinking of her friends and the Big Bend tablet, she wrote to the McGees in February, suggesting that Dr. Fell might take an interest. Neither Miriam nor the McGees had ever heard of Dr. Fell. But after nearly two decades of waiting, the speed of his response was breathtaking — less than three months.

Having asked Cyclone Covey in late April to sound out Dr. Fell, Bernice wrote to Miriam early in July, "I am so excited I could burst!!! The Big Bend tablet has been recognized and deciphered!"

Dr. Covey sent a photocopy of Dr. Fell's note to Bernice, and in his letter exclaimed, "Your labors are paying off!" As for language, Dr. Fell declared the message to be "written illiterately in Iberic language, using debased Roman-Iberic script with some *Magtinil*-letter, and lines 5 and 6 deliberately written in Iberic, Lycian, and Lydian (for added efficacy). Date — ca. 302 A.D. (?)." Though his primary translation was "provisional," as he noted, in the long run he saw fit to make no change in his wording of the inscription.

About two thousand years ago, the language groups named by Dr. Fell were subjects of the Roman Empire, then at its zenith. All three belonged to maritime regions with huge fleets and advanced navigational skills. Iberia is an ancient name for Spain, derived from the river Liberus, now the Ebro, which separated Roman from Carthaginian possessions. The Iberian alphabet, said Dr. Fell, evolved "from a Phoenician way of writing." Lycia, a country in Asia Minor whose southern boundary was the Mediterranean, was once conquered by the Lydians, thus mixing those peoples and their languages. Lydia has been called "a celebrated kingdom" of Asia Minor bordering the Aegaean Sea. The first coinage of gold and silver and the first public games are said to have occurred in Lydia. Early in the Christian era, these three regions were subject to Roman cultural and linguistic influence.

Where did this group of apparent Iberians, Lycians, and Lydians think they were going when they found themselves at Hot Springs, Texas? Had they taken a wrong turn, hoping to join comrades on the Cimarron or the Arkansas? Had they crossed the Pacific and come across the West? Were they prospectors? If so, had they detected the rich silver deposits near Boquillas? Were they sick or dying?

Whatever their mission or circumstance, a sort of ritual is implied in the Big Bend tablet, as somebody took a sharp instrument and on an earthen slab clearly wrote these words of prayer, with a dotted line across the middle:

> Why (this) suffering?
> Ah, what anguish!
> A call to prayer — 29th December
> First winter month — Year 6
> Heal us! [Iberic]
> Heal us! [Lycian] Heal us! [Lydian]
> . . . .
> The faithful by sorrows are beset;
> O guide us, Mithras.
> Show forth thy power and
> the promises of aid as
> revealed by Ahura-
> Mazda.
> > Amen.

It appears that a party of ancients representing three language groups were pleading to Mithras for mercy. In those days Mithraism was extremely popular throughout the Roman Empire and was a strong rival of Christianity, with which it shares many parallels, including absolution by baptism. The birthday of Mithras, for example, is December 25 and may have been observed at Hot Springs. Also Mithras is a god of truth, light, and brotherly love; his visible symbol, the sun. Opposing him is the god of falsehood, darkness, and evil (the devil). Mithraism is derived from the teachings of a Persian, Zoroaster, who was inspired with revelations given to him by Ahura-Mazda, the "one, true, indescribable god." The tenets of Mithraism are contained in a book called the *Avesta*. And here at Hot Springs, it would appear, were devout Zoroastrians, who as Dr. Cyclone Covey had surmised, may have come down the Rio Grande from New Mexico.

The nature of the Big Bend tablet's message was gratifying to Donald Uzzell. It was sometime after finding the artifact, he said, that "I learned that in some countries they have what is called a 'prayer wall,' with holes that they stick prayers in."

The skeptical park rangers and the early "experts" who scoffed at the Big Bend tablet were only a few of many who profess doubt as to its authenticity. Among conventional archaeologists there is considerable resistance to virtually all epigraphic discoveries and claims. Willingness to consider them with some objectivity has grown more in Europe than in America, and there, more among linguists than archaeologists.

Dr. J. Charles Kelley, an archaeologist now of Fort Davis, acknowledged that too many of his profession refuse to consider new concepts that might alter the well-established version of the origin of human habitation in the Americas. He mentioned a former director of the Smithsonian Institution who refused to accept any epigraphic artifacts whatsoever for study or display in his domain. Many seem to dismiss epigraphers as eccentrics, classing their inscriptions as fraud, fake, and forgery — or as imaginative misinterpretation.

Dr. Kelley professed that he had objectively considered several presentations by epigraphers. He knew of evidence — which epigraphers have evaluated — that the Los Lunas Ten Commandments might be a forgery perpetrated by college students in the 1930s. Epigraphers, however, also point to a report that Indians led a rancher to the stone in 1871 and showed it to him.

"But most convincing to me," said Dr. Kelley, "that there could not have been Europeans in America before Columbus,

is that morphological studies of Indian remains show no evidence of European diseases. The Indians were extremely vulnerable to them."

It seems that even epigraphers are forced to give the Big Bend tablet an ambiguous rating. With about ninety percent chance of accurate translation, thus "saying what it presents," the text might rate at the top as "Highly Probable." On the other hand, the nonexistence of the tablet reduces its rating to the lowest category, "Possible." Only the Nickles photograph and the written account by the skeptical David Evan stand as testimony that there ever was such a tablet.

Other factors also make epigraphers cautious. No comparable inscriptions or artifacts as yet have been recognized in the same region — with one possible exception in the unusual petroglyph that Miriam pointed out. Bernice McGee discovered the axe in the glyph is "a symbol of a Roman deity associated with Ahura-Mazda."

Epigraphers also ask how it was weathered. The apparent

lack of weathering was the feature that caused doubt in the first park ranger to see it. The thing "looked new" to him. Donald reported that the fragments were indeed in very good condition, except for eroded edges on the three or four most exposed to the elements. He went on to say, "I don't understand how the tablet could have disintegrated back there in the old park headquarters. I didn't feel like it had any tendency to crumble, because the pieces felt rock hard. I believe that if I could find the old dump where they threw it, I might could find some pieces today. I don't care what kind of weather they've been out in."

So what was it made of and how? As amateur investigators, the McGees decided that the tablet was made of a natural cake of "bentonite," a durable mud common in Tornillo Creek and elsewhere in the Big Bend. And that it must have held fast in almost perfect condition for more than sixteen hundred years in its still, dry hiding place. Or would it?

Geologist Dr. Frank W. Daugherty, now of Alpine, pointed out that the Tornillo Creek mud is not pure bentonite, as it contains "both swelling and non-swelling clay, as well as silt and sand." Even pure bentonite, he said, which swells when wet, will shrink to its original size when the water evaporates. "Thus," he said, "a tablet made of bentonite would disintegrate rather rapidly in a dry and hot environment."

But if it were new, what sort of person could have forged it, writing in forgotten script in three long dead European languages, having found or made a durable earthen slab of some kind to scratch it on? And with what? Then breaking it into fragments and storing it in an almost invisible niche on a bluff near the mouth of Tornillo Creek?

Could Donald Uzzell have done it—or any of the party he was traveling with? Could he possibly have written a Mithran prayer? In 1990 he was put to questions in something like a cross-examination.

> *Q:* What is the nature and extent of your education?
> *A:* I had a high school education—graduated from San Mar-

cos High School. Before that I attended Baptist Military Academy in San Marcos. The only other training would be law enforcement. I worked as a reserve deputy in Bastrop under then Sheriff Jimmy Nutt.

Q: Have you acquired the skill to write in the languages of the Big Bend tablet?

A: No. At times it's hard enough to write the English language, much less try for a dead language that I for one am not familiar with. No, I could not possibly have written any of this.

Q: Before or since December, 1961, have you known anyone who possibly could have written it?

A: No.

Q: What is your reaction to the fact that some authorities, especially archaeologists, believe the Big Bend tablet to be a hoax?

A: If it is a hoax, my family and I are not a part of it. And if it is a hoax, someone went to a great length to hide the tablet in the cliff.

Q: What was your profession in 1961?

A: I owned and operated a TV leasing company, leasing TV's to several hospitals in Texas, only. I started this business in the late '50's and sold it in 1984. Before that I worked for Dow Chemical in Freeport. I lived in San Marcos from 1961 to 1963, moved to Austin, then to Bastrop in 1969.

Right now I'm located in Brownsville. I own and operate Border Machinery, and handle the passing of equipment made in the States that has been bought by Mexican nationals. I hold a lot of it on about ten acres I have, while getting permits to deliver it in Mexico.

It seems that neither the Uzzells nor the Nickleses had the ability, much less the desire, to inscribe a translatable Mithran prayer on a soft but hardening slab and then tuck it away at Hot Springs. Nor did they know anybody who could. The only suspect seems to have been an unknown Iberian writing about A.D. 300, far away from home in the Big Bend.

When Dr. Fell reproduced the Big Bend tablet and remarked on it in *Saga America* (1980), the artifact discovered by Donald Uzzell took its place in the spectrum of recorded American and world history. Just as the tablet was found as an assortment of jigsaw pieces, it has now become one of the thousands of epigraphic pieces from all over the American continents to be fit together by scholars — specialists seeking to explain the presence and purpose of early European, North African, and Asian visitors in the Western Hemisphere since, they claim, at least three thousand years before Christ.

12.

Cowboys and God

Last night as I lay on the prairie
And looked at the stars in the sky,
I wondered if ever a cowboy
Would drift to that sweet bye and bye.
—"A Cowboy's Dream"

ON A SUNDAY MORNING, a cowboy woke up on the bar of a deserted saloon. Still a little drunk from his Saturday night howl, he stumbled out to his horse at the hitching rail and headed for camp.

On the edge of the cowtown he came to a church house surrounded by horses and buggies. Joyous hymn singing spilled out the windows. The cowboy tethered his horse, went in, and stood at the back bench. He joined in lustily on "Throw Out the Lifeline" and "Standing on the Promises."

Then the parson intoned, "Let us bow our heads in prayer."

The cowboy spoke up, "Hell, no! Let's sing some more."

This legendary cowboy's religious sentiment was more spontaneous than decorous. His religion did not interfere with his being himself or speaking his own language. What religion he had told him to be a square shooter and to expect no less of the next fellow. In worship he preferred music and poetry, or even silence, to palaver.

The saying "There is no law west of the Pecos, and no God west of El Paso" was not quite true. In the absence of churches, religious training was up to the family. In widely scattered ranch houses, parents read the Bible to their children, answered their questions as best they could, and sang hymns as well as secular songs. From these families came both cowboys and badmen. (John Wesley Hardin's father was a Methodist circuit rider.) Perhaps the only regular ceremony was offering thanks before meals.

That was the practice of Charles Goodnight in both Texas and New Mexico. It is said that he once received a couple of cowboys to his table for a noon meal before they drifted on their way. When he asked one of them to say grace, the startled waddie was tongue-tied. Then he blurted out:

> Lord, help us to be able
> To eat all that's on the table,
> And if there's more in the kitchen
> Send it out a-pitchin'.

Goodnight took no offense. Without change of expression he followed the parody with a short prayer, and the meal began.

Though a cowboy could be mischievous and sometimes profane, he meant no harm. Moral and religious in a simple way, he saw no use in talking about God, much less Jesus Christ. If he were to be properly branded and marked by conversion and baptism, ministers had to come to him — and some did. The most effective were circuit riders with genuine cow-country experience.

There were many such men. Texas Methodist Brother Jack Potter was a professional gambler before he was a preacher. Baptist Brother H. K. Stimson of Kansas was a stagecoach driver. Brother W. W. James had been a cowboy. In 1918 Christian Brother H. M. Bandy of Marfa, Texas, stumbled into the Brite Ranch headquarters besieged by Mexican revolutionary bandits. Having lived and fought through Indian troubles, he said a prayer, took a rifle, and filled his pockets with bullets (but no more shooting occurred). Methodist Bishop Asbury advised his missionaries in the West, "Leave all your vain speculation and metaphysical reasoning behind."

Perhaps the most colorful Texas cowboy preacher was Baptist Brother Leonard R. "Lallie" Millican, who worked the range — especially in the Big Bend — from 1879 until his death in 1938. In his prime he was a lanky, bony-featured six-footer with gray eyes, wavy hair, and a semi-walrus mustache. In his speech and sermon delivery, he was solemnly, urgently sincere.

As a young cowboy near Lampasas, he said he loved "bunking with a real outfit, rounding up, cutting, branding, and marking calves. I liked the clean, wild life of the men who went straight, did honest work for small wages, and spent their earnings like millionaires — men who stood by each other through thick and thin. With them it was a six-shooter for a turncoat, and a limb and rope for a horse thief."

At seventeen Lallie joined the vigilante Anti-Horse Thief League, but, he said, "I absolutely refused to help hang anyone." He wanted a rustler to stand trial. In the years before his conversion, he recalled, "I had some remarkable experiences on the frontier of Texas with horse thieves and outlaws. I often wonder how I came out alive."

Cut out to be a lawman, eighteen-year-old Lallie was appointed Lampasas County deputy sheriff and served for three years. Those who knew him said he was utterly fearless. As lawman and later as preacher, he, unarmed, took pistols out of the hands of men who were ready to use them. Riding in a stagecoach on a church mission in New Mexico, he wrestled down an obnoxious drunk who was harassing female passengers and sat on him until they reached their destination. Though he never drank, Lallie was often in saloons, because he enjoyed the companionship.

It was not easy for a cowboy to modify that special comradeship was his "pards." At twenty-one Lallie was converted at a camp meeting and vowed to be a Baptist preacher. Reminiscing, he said, "It was hard for me to say, 'Thy will be done.'"

As it turned out, Brother Lallie was close to West Texas cowboys the rest of his life and remained one himself. He acquired a little ranch near Van Horn, loved to work cattle and especially to break horses. First, however, he attended Baylor University (then at Independence, Texas) to become a Baptist home missionary—circuit rider—for the entire prairie, mountain, and desert country from San Angelo to El Paso. That distance of almost five hundred miles was limited otherwise by the New Mexico line and the Rio Grande. His parish was the entire Big Bend country and then some.

His mission was simple but arduous. To comfort, convert, and baptize, he went by horseback or hack cross-country to ranch families at home and their hired cowboys in camp. In these lonely places, a visitor was always welcome and a preacher somebody special, if not a curiosity. Brother Lallie helped to organize village churches and camp meetings. He traveled, he said, "in all kinds of weather—through rain, storm, sleet, and snow, as well as fair weather, with only a saddle blanket for a bed, a saddle for a pillow, and the heavens for a covering."

In churchless Pecos, he held "a good meeting," he said, "in a saloon, using card and billiard tables for seats, one card table as a pulpit or book box." He held a camp meeting in the Davis Mountains for "fifteen days without a song, as no one could sing, and baptized fifteen."

Millican's dedication to his work gave him little time at home with his wife, Georgia, and their children. In his brief "Life Sketch," he gave her full credit for managing their business affairs.

Old-timers in the Texas Big Bend country still laugh about Brother Lallie's outlaw horses and mules. "In the early years of my ministry," he said, "I went always on horseback, sometimes breaking in a bronc for its use in my work." Often he was straddled over a wall-eyed snorter that would kick at him, bite him, or jerk loose from him as he dismounted. He kept a hitching rope noosed around his animal's neck, with the coil tied to the saddle horn. Before swinging out of the saddle, he uncoiled the rope and expertly threw a couple of half hitches around a post. Then he would slide off down the horse's hind legs.

Part of Brother Lallie's mission was to give away books, Bibles,

and tracts. Draped over his mean horse was a pair of oversized saddlebags, each pocket made to hold a twenty-four-pound sack of flour. Into these the parson crammed books and pamphlets. Sometimes his horse would loco — buck like a grasshopper, set the saddle bags to flapping, fill the air with books and papers, and strew them all over the pasture. Envigorated by the contest, Brother Lallie sat tight in the saddle, fanning the outlaw with his big Stetson until the bucking stopped. Then he would say, "Boys, that's the best distribution I ever had."

The cowpokes in camp roared with laughter, took him as "one of the boys," and helped him pick up and reload the bags.

Like other true cowboys, Brother Lallie never complained of injury or pain. Random accidents, it is said, broke nearly every bone in his body. Chills and fever could hardly stop him. When he finally owned an automobile, he drove it the way he urged his broncs, bouncing wildly over the roughest country. By merely driving his car, he once broke four ribs, and later ruptured himself cranking it.

For about twenty years, starting in 1890, Brother Lallie was a regular among the preachers at the well-known interdenominational Bloys Cowboy Camp Meeting in the Davis Mountains. Sometimes he highlighted a sermon with cow-work images. To illustrate how breaking only one point of God's law is to break all of it (James 2:10), he said, "Cattle in a pen awaiting shipment break down one gate and scatter all over the country. They are as much out of it as if they had broken every gate and every panel to splinters."

The story of at least one cowboy's conversion at Bloys survives in a tale told by Joe M. Evans. It was past a cold midnight, and several cowmen still sat around a campfire. One cowpoke from a roundup camp was elated about his conversion that Sunday. He said, "Boys, I won't hear no more preachin' till next year. I want to do this thing up right." He insisted that he be baptized immediately.

It had turned cold and rainy that day, and the creek was running with barely enough water to dunk a cowboy. Lighting their way with kerosene lanterns, they rousted Brother Lallie out of a sound sleep in his tent. Wearing only his slicker, he joined the boys. The cowboy sat on the creek bank and shucked off his clothes. Then he and the parson waded into the ice-water as floating hail stones swirled around their legs. With simple prayer and ceremonial words, Brother Millican immersed his man. There must have been jovial talk before Brother Lallie returned to his tent. The cowboy pulled on his clothes, got on his horse, and rode twenty miles to his camp for roundup work at sunup.

In his last years, Millican's long dream of an annual West Texas Baptist camp meeting came true. In Paisano Pass on the old Chihuahua Trail between Alpine and Marfa lies the Paisano Baptist Encampment ground. In a forest of live oaks, it is surrounded by cliffs and mountains. Though dedicated to Paisano, he still gave time to the Bloys camp meeting.

Before he died in 1938, Millican helped to establish and build many Baptist churches in far West Texas, including at least two for Hispanics. He initiated a camp meeting for his Hispanic *va-*

quero brethren at Paisano, but it failed for lack of attendance. He served at least three terms as a county commissioner and regularly attended the Texas State Democratic conventions, as well as Baptist conventions. He was active in both the Texas and National Cattlemen's Associations, serving as chaplain for both. At the Texas State Legislature he was an effective lobbyist for Texas cattlemen, of which he was one. Millican's story is fully told by Katy Stokes in her book, *Paisano: The Story of a Cowboy and a Camp Meeting.*

The Paisano Baptist Encampment has convened annually since 1922, and in 1988 the attendance was reported to be about twenty-five hundred. Brother Lallie and Georgia are buried on the grounds. Their two sons died of disease in early manhood. Near the tabernacle stands an obelisk to call attention to one of the cowboy preachers who brought God west of the Pecos.

Many a drifting cowboy was a better candidate for salvation than his roughhouse reputation might suggest. One of these was a whiskery line rider who was gone from his line shack all summer, rounding up strays and branding calves missed in the spring roundup. When he returned, he was puzzled by horses, buggies, and hacks standing around his cabin. Homesteaders had moved in, and a circuit rider was holding church.

The cowboy entered and sat with the people. Coming to the invitation, the preacher pled, "Stand up for Jesus! Isn't there a single Christian? Nobody here that loves Jesus? If you do, please rise."

When the cowboy glanced around and saw that everybody was bored, he stood up. The preacher exclaimed, "I'm glad there's one Christian here. Tell us your experience. Tell us what you know about Jesus."

The cowboy said, "I never heard of him in my life. But I'll stand up for any feller that ain't got no more friends than what this Jesus has."

That cow-camp yarn says that many a drifting, open-range cowboy was a working Christian, even if he did not know it. Recalling his Davis Mountains cow work of 1893, when he was ten, Joe M. Evans of El Paso said, "These cowboys, with all their faults, were big hearted and always kind to a little boy." If a horse threw Joe or he landed on a cactus, they picked him up, consoled him, and pulled out the thorns. Sometimes they stood his night guard and let him sleep. These were, he said, "the hardest men to be found anywhere—wicked, sinful, cussin' characters who told dirty stories—some even outlaws on the dodge. I learned to love them."

In later years, as a New Mexico rancher and Baptist lay preacher, Evans founded several Ranchmen's Camp Meetings in western states. On the open range near Fort Davis, Texas, he was reared in a literate, Christian home—at times only a tent or a dugout. In 1889 at age six, he went with his family to the first interdenominational Bloys Cowboy Camp Meeting six thousand feet up in the Davis Mountains. With several ranch couples and their broods camped nearby, Joe slept in the wagon bed with his mother, while older boys and the men bedded under their tarps on the ground. He had never had as many playmates before—of the fifty-eight people there, twenty-three were children. (In 1988 an attendance of three thousand was reported.)

For the rest of his life Joe never missed the August week at Bloys if he could help it. In old age he said, "When I die and go to heaven and time for Bloys camp meeting comes around, I'm afraid I'll want to run off and come back to it."

Unlike his "true cowboy" Baptist colleague Lallie, William B. Bloys, Presbyterian, had to learn to be a cowboy preacher. A Tennessee farm boy born in 1847, he taught in local schools, worked his way through an Ohio seminary, and along the way became a skilled carpenter and cabinet maker. In 1879 he was assigned to Coleman, Texas, as a circuit rider to serve the open range from there to El Paso, six hundred miles west. He preached his first Texas sermon in a Coleman saloon.

In West Texas he learned to attract cowboys to God by riding out to cow camps and ranch houses. Of medium height and wearing a brushy mustache, he had a sturdy build that concealed weak lungs. His health, damaged by his riding and sleeping out in rough weather, compelled him to accept the pastorate of the mile-high Fort Davis church. He persisted, nevertheless, in rigorous circuit riding.

From a spark struck by Baptist ranching couple Zack and Exa Means, the Bloys Cowboy Camp Meeting flared to life. When William Bloys once stopped overnight at the Crow's Nest (the Means's ranch house) they suggested such a meeting and its permanent place, Skillman Grove, a clump of live oaks on a flat in the Davis Mountains. On the Overland Trail, the place was central to widely scattered ranches and distant villages. Several families would camp there for a few days and offer free food to all who strayed in, with Bloys leading the main services. Among the first six families were those of the Means and of George and Kate Evans, parents of Joe and Will.

In duplication of a southern custom dating to the early 1800s, a camp meeting involved several processes: (1) spreading word up and down wagon roads and cow trails; (2) loading up for camp and getting there; (3) scheduling religious services; (4) working to build and maintain facilities, not counting food preparation; and (5) relaxing between and after work periods and services.

Announcement of the event spread by mouth as ranchmen or their cowboys rode on ordinary business between cow camps, ranch houses, and villages like Fort Davis, Alpine, Marathon, Kent, Marfa, and Van Horn.

For the families to get themselves to the grounds was a social adventure that broke their year-long isolation. Extremely important in instigating a camp meeting were the ranch women, who not only urged it on the men, but toiled to bake pies, cakes, and bread to take along. With seventy-five or hundred miles to go, some families headed out days in advance, spending two or three nights with other families along the dim wagon road. By the second day's travel, processions had formed of wagons, buggies, and hacks for the women and girls, with men and boys on horseback.

If there was a fiddler in the bunch, there were nightly dances at successive ranch houses.

The morning after an overnight visit often was an uproar. Joe M. Evans recalled that in saddling and hitching up, "horses pitched off their riders, wagon tongues broke out, harness were torn up, horses were loose with saddles on, and mothers cried and prayed, while us boys were really having fun. It looked like a three-ring circus."

As the processions joined at Skillman Grove, families chose their camp sites, and a hundred years later, some of their descendants have permanent camp houses built on those very spots. The animals were turned loose to graze at will. Men hauled water from a shallow, spring-fed creek and chopped wood for the fires. While women organized their camps and outdoor kitchens, men rode out and shot antelope to supplement beef brought from home. Stragglers rode in, singly or in pairs, especially for the Sunday sessions.

At mealtime the women cooked in iron skillets and Dutch ovens, while the men did some barbecuing. Home-baked goods were warmed up, including biscuits made with bear grease. The families camped at Bloys were—and still are—prepared to feed all comers gratis. Nowadays, however, contributions are appreciated.

After a year or two, the ranchmen brought chuck wagons and Mexican camp cooks, thus relieving their wives of considerable work. There is no record that any of these cooks ever attended or were invited to services.

To succeeding Bloys encampments, some families brought tents, some of which provided little more comfort than the out-of-doors. Evans recalled, "When it rained, we all got wet, unless we rolled up our beds, put on our slickers, and sat on our bed rolls until it quit." Every night, rain or moonshine, Brother Bloys lit his coal oil lantern and made the rounds. Often he divided his quilts with a lone cowboy unprepared to stay the night. If a cowboy could be kept on the grounds, he might be won for the Lord.

There were and are at least five services a day at Bloys, including daily morning and night preaching services. At the 1889 encampment, somebody produced an Arbuckle coffee shipping crate for Brother Bloys to preach from in the open air. Bloys picked fresh wildflowers and arranged them in a glass of water to adorn his "Bible box," a custom he followed as long as he lived. After the first camp meeting, preaching duties were shared by many others, notably Brother Millican and the renowned Baptist Dr. George W. Truett of Dallas.

Between services men and older boys constructed an arbor and kept it in repair. To build the arbor, they cut posts and rafters from longleaf pines in the mountains. Having secured them in the loop of a lasso, they pulled them into camp behind their horses. They repeated the process with brush for the roof. In later years a secondhand, one-ring circus tent was acquired, to be succeeded by a permanent tabernacle with a concrete floor. Brother Bloys supervised the construction of backed benches and built a handsome lectern that is used today. Most western camp meetings have grown along the same line. No work, however, was allowed on Sunday, except for the cooks.

While the work was going on, the smaller children galloped about on stick horses, roped stumps, and climbed mountains. Boys and sometimes girls played at "branding calves," chasing, roping, and throwing each other to the ground. Occasionally, fathers would romp along with them.

There was recreation for all. "After the night services," said Evans, "we got around some of the camps and sang and told stories and drank coffee until a late hour." Preachers joined in the jovial camp fire circles. The Evans family brought their black bronc-buster Old Jake, who sang, shuffle-danced, and preached brief, traditional Negro sermons. Another family brought horsebreaker and songster Febronio Calanche and his guitar. There were also "break-down" fiddler Pat Spruell and a Gillett couple who performed a duet with guitar.

After the older folks and younger children were in their bedrolls, young people, some in couples, walked into the moonlit hills. Drifting into sleep, their elders heard far away laughter and voices in song. At dawn the cooks cleaned up utensils used by the youngsters in a midnight snack.

Despite the romantic song making in the night, one rancher said that the sweetest music he ever heard at Bloys was the distant after-midnight baying of a pack of dogs on the heels of a fox or wolf.

On the Monday morning departure, loading up to go home was easier than getting the horses and mules back in harness or under saddle. They had grown fat by grazing loose for a week and were mighty frisky. The dust was flying as yelling men gathered the remuda in a rope corral and lassoed out the balky animals for each other. Sometimes two men had to rope a horse — head and heel. "They would stretch him out if he didn't behave," Evans said. Also, after a week of piety and resolution, "It was hard to keep from cussin' when a mule kicked you or your horse bucked you off. The bad part was we had to stir up enough religion to last us twelve months."

Homeward bound, the caravans of families became progressively smaller. Repeated were overnight stops at wayside ranch houses. Though there may have been dancing again, now there were baptizings in nearby dirt tanks.

Some of these baptizings were especially memorable. At a stock tank, the travelers joined in song and prayer, and Brother Millican presided with appropriate words. Then a blind man fell eight feet — unhurt — into a dry well. The boys and girls could not stifle their giggles. Next, said Evans, "a jackass cut loose with a bray that echoed down the canyon."

Somewhat deaf, Millican was unaware, but he knew that something was disrupting the ceremony. When the next group of converts walked into the water, said Evans, "here came a bunch of mules and horses." They also waded in less than a hundred feet from the baptizing, slurped long draughts of water and flopped down to wallow in a splattering mud bath. When the animals left, one thirsty mule drank on until her sides bulged out. When she found herself alone, she ran after the other mules, turning her nose to one side then the other and splitting all ears with a hee-haw every time she hit the ground.

"She left one of the best audiences she will ever have," said Evans. "We couldn't hold it. We had to laugh, baptising or no baptising." The humor may have been welcome to Brother Millican, as he burst out with laughter also.

The family farthest away reached home alone. In their accustomed isolation, they unloaded and got back to the business of tending the cattle, horses, and barnyard chickens and cows. Their cup was brimmed with spiritual renewal, supported by the immense pleasure of a week-long party and semi-rodeo. They did not have to mark the calendar to be all set for next year's cowboy camp meeting.

Each day during a Bloys Camp Meeting, besides morning and night sermons, there are several smaller groups sessions. Today many a rancher and cowboy is proud of a daily prayer meeting held at five in the afternoon under the "Men's Prayer Tree," a stately live oak. The custom is derived from the southern practice of separate men's and women's "Grove Meetings" before each evening's service, which no preacher may attend. The Men's Prayer Tree also has been called the "Grove Tree" and the "Cowboy's Hitchin' Post." For some years at Bloys there was also a men's once-a-week Confessional Prayer Meeting that more often was called the "Come Clean Meeting."

Tales are still told about what went on at some of the preachings and supplementary services. Before 1900 a rancher brought ten hunting dogs to Bloys. They ate well on antelope meat scraps at various family kitchens. One night in the glow of lanterns under the tent top, Brother Bloys was mid-sermon. Ranchmen, wives, children, and cowboys sat attentively. Suddenly, all the hounds set to barking and baying. A wildcat raced by the tent in plain sight of the congregation with the yowling dogs right on his tail. Then the men and boys came plowing out between the crowded benches to take up the chase.

Soon they had the cat treed but could not shake him down.

A boy ran barefoot back to camp and fetched a rifle. Pow! In moments the tail-wagging dogs followed the grinning men back to the congregation to show off their dead wildcat.

Dr. Bloys was not smiling. Though he always took part in after-sermon campfire fun, he tolerated no foolishness where God's business was concerned. At the next morning's service, his first words were, "There will be no more dogs allowed on this campground." The rancher and his hounds rode out that day.

According to Joe M. Evans, a successful service was held at a Ranchmen's Camp Meeting in New Mexico in the 1940s. Under a tent top, Dr. George W. Truett had finished a powerful sermon and was uttering a prayer in advance of the invitation. As it turned out, no invitation was needed. A shirt-sleeved, open-collared cowboy got up and clanked down front in his boots and spurs. Without a word he seized Dr. Truett by the hand, mid-prayer. "It broke up the prayer meeting," Evans said, "but it started a revival."

Cowboys came down front from all over the tent and many from the dark outside, "too wild" to sit hemmed in. Some were over forty and had never been to church in their lives. Twenty-two cowpokes were converted that night. One of the ranch hands went to his pal in the audience, put an arm around him, and begged him to join his buddies in Christ. Tears poured down his face when he noticed four or five walking down the middle aisle at once. In his enthusiasm, he all but shouted, "I believe the whole damn outfit is goin' to join the church!"

The Men's Prayer Tree became a standby of cowboy camp meetings established in the 1940s by Joe Evans at Capitan and Magdalena, New Mexico; at Prescott, Arizona; and in Wyoming, eight thousand feet up in the Rockies and a hundred fifty miles from Cheyenne.

At the first of the Bloys Prayer Tree meetings in 1890, ranchmen brought their sons, sat in a circle, and meant to talk about God and His goodness. The ranchman selected as leader called on the men one by one to say something, but every man shook his head and remained silent. These were reverent cattlemen, but as Will F. Evans (Joe's brother) said, "Their feelings were too deep for human utterance."

After the second unsuccessful meeting, the ranch wives broke down the reticence. They sent their little boys prepared to recite short pieces from the Bible.

Not to be outdone, one of the men told of his miraculous escape from injury or death — perhaps being bitten by a rattlesnake or almost bucked off over a cliff. It seems that the men's prayer tree service then became a kind of yarn swapping with a religious theme. Captain James B. Gillett, Marfa rancher and former Texas Ranger, told of his scrapes with murderous Indians or gunslingers and how it must have been the Lord that pulled him through. During the wars in Europe, the Pacific, Korea, and Vietnam, many young men overseas got word that they were remembered under the Prayer Tree.

The Men's Prayer Tree was credited by Joe Evans for the fact that for the first thirty-five years of the county's existence, not one Fort Davis person was sent to the penitentiary. And for an eleven-year stretch, there was not one Jeff Davis County grand jury indictment. "It has done more good," he believed, "than all the law enforcements."

As for the "Come Clean" sessions, Joe Evans said, "We called it a prayer meeting, but it was better than any show you ever went to." On a midweek night after the sermon, ranchmen and cowboys gathered around a little fire.

One vividly remembered star of these gatherings was ranchman Henry B. Mayfield, known as "Ole Mass." Five of Henry's ranching and hunting friends prayed for this kindly, mischievous reprobate for twenty-five years. Nobody in the Big Bend Country knew much about him, except that he was a great storyteller, a natural-born cusser, and a professed infidel. He never talked about his life before 1885, when he drove his herd from near San Angelo to the open range of the Davis Mountains. Late in life he let it out that he was a Confederate veteran. When rancher friends annually urged him to attend the local Bloys Cowboy

Camp Meeting, he objected, "Hell, no! I might get religion."

Of average height, Mayfield resembled William F. "Buffalo Bill" Cody. Judging by his dress and stance in hunting trip snapshots, he must have cultivated that image. As a theatrical yarn spinner, he acted out roles in his stories. He was called "Old Mass," because he reminded friends of an old time southern colonel. Consequently, he called his wife "Ole Miss" and delighted in teasing her.

He raised cattle and kept hunting dogs. Often, he dug for the gold he was certain lay under his spread, and more than once he packed into Mexico in vain effort to strike it rich. Several prospectors enjoyed his grubstake, only to wind up empty handed. Ole Mass always seemed broke.

Like other cowmen, he was hospitable. He would greet a guest, booming out, "Git down and come on in! Ole Miss'll cook up some of old Zack Means's beef I stole the other day."

As a hunter and trapper, his skill in woodcraft was said to be unsurpassed. Paradoxically, it was to hunt that he appeared sometimes with his dogs at Bloys Camp Meeting. He would bring his wife, get her set up in camp, and then disappear on horseback for a week, his dogs trotting around him. More often, sons or friends would bring Ole Miss to Bloys, as she tried never to skip.

Ole Mass was a practical joker. Once when he and his family were gone, along came Joe Evans and Sam Means after a day rounding up strays.

They called out, "Ole Mass!"

No answer.

After penning their horses and feeding them from Ole Mass's crib, they cooked supper, spent the night, and next morning headed out with their cows. They met Ole Mass on his way home.

"Howdy, Mass. We stayed all night with you last night, but you wasn't there."

Mass said, "Boys, I shore am sorry as hell I wasn't there. I'm afraid you didn't find a damn thing to eat."

"Oh, we ate good. We had plenty of that jerky you have hanging on the line."

Ole Mass put on a horrified face. He seemed unnerved. "Boys!" he exclaimed. "That meat was from a damned old coyote! I had it hanging up there for my dogs. Why, that'll make you sick as a horse!"

Joe and Sam had not ridden a mile before they relieved their nausea in the brush. Back at the ranch Old Mass was laughing, and he laughed again over the years as he reminded his friends of that perfectly good beef jerky.

Though he finally took to hanging around the Bloys campground without his dogs, Ole Mass refused to attend service. His friends said he was just plain mule-headed and would not go because they wanted him to. Eventually he broke down, went to a daytime service, and seized an opportunity for outrageousness.

On the back bench he sat solemnly in his majestic Buffalo Bill presence beside a string of mischievous giggling boys squirming and pinching each other. Brother Bloys started his sermon. From the rear a woman walked in with her pet screw-tail bull terrier at her heels.

Ole Mass could not resist. He reached down and straightened out the dog's tail with a yank. Will Evans wrote, "That dog spoke right out in meeting and nearly lifted the brush off the arbor."

Brother Bloys stopped. He glared at the back row. Ole Mass sat solemnly erect. At his elbow the boys were doubled over, howling with laughter. Somehow, Brother Bloys cut the service back onto the trail and headed it home.

It's always been a rule at Bloys that no business transactions of any kind are made, but Ole Mass played a con game there, all in fun.

Two of the Evans boys, Rube and Ell, had been playing in their make believe branding pens. They were barefoot and dirty, with clothes twisted and hair tangled. Ole Mass approached a visiting couple from New York with a doleful story about these orphan outcasts. The New York lady opened her purse and handed him a five-dollar bill.

"Now," she said, "you just go buy something for those poor children."

Gravely, Ole Mass swept off his hat, took the money, and thanked the lady for her mercy to the unfortunate. When he got out of her sight, he commenced a week-long laugh about it.

It was at Bloys in 1920 that Henry B. Mayfield, at age seventy-five, came to God. The camp meeting over, a caravan on the way home assembled at a dirt tank on a nearby ranch for a baptizing. Baptist Brother Leonard R. Millican presided.

Before he waded into the water, Ole Mass surveyed the bunch with his steel-gray eyes. He made a little speech:

"There's somethin' I want to say to these people here. Just because I've sopped gravy out of the same skillet for forty years with George Evans and Zack Means is not why I'm joinin' the Baptist church. I'm joinin' because I like it!"

Upon his conversion Ole Mass told the boys that he was going to quit cussing, because he did not think it right for a church member to cuss. The very next year he "came clean" with the boys. A natural-born actor and elocutionist, he confessed to a spell of cussing.

He had been cleaning out his cow pen, he said, with a scraper and a team of cranky mules. The job went well until the scraper caught on a rock. Ole Mass yanked the reins but the mules kept going. They jerked him down, his boot strap hung on the scraper, and the mules dragged him around in the filth two or three times before his boot came off.

"I didn't try to git up," he said. "I set there in that mess and I asked the Lord to let me have a recess jest long enough to tell them blankety-blank mules what I thought of 'em."

Then Ole Mass made yet another confession. He had promised to pray for the five—including Joe and Will Evans—every night, because they led him to the Lord. He began by saying,

"Boys, I prayed for every one of you every night at nine o'clock, except for one time."

An avid hunter, he had jumped at the invitation to join a neighbor in tracking down a panther that killed one of his colts. Ole Mass hurriedly assembled his weapons and bedroll, put some grub together, hitched up his hack, and loaded on his dogs. He started out on his long night's journey, mountain lion on his mind. As he moved through the dark, nine-thirty came along. He stopped the mules right there, got out and down on his knees, and implored, "Lord, please forgive me for not praying for my boys."

Later at a men's "Come Clean" confessional at Bloys, he admitted to another relapse that involved his favorite horse. Big all over, gentle Old Roan stood about seventeen hands high and was never known to pitch. According to Will Evans, Old Mass said:

> Boys, you know that China tree down on the flat? Well, s'I, 'I'll jist go down there and set out a couple of traps for an ole coyote that's been pesterin' me.' S'I, 'He'll shore come smellin' around that old tree purty damn pronto.' S'I, 'I'll saddle up ole Roan and set them traps right away,' and that's what I done.
>
> Then next mornin', s'I, 'I'll git on ole Roan and go see what I got.' And shore 'nough, when I got to that old tree, I seen I had the ole wolf by one front foot. But boys, I'd gone off and forgot my gun. I knowed where a club was, up in the fork of that ole tree, so I tied ole Roan and eased up to the tree and got the club. S'I, 'I shore don't want him to break a paw and git away,' so I slipped up as close as I could and whaled that ole wolf over the head and laid him out.
>
> S'I, 'He's deader'n a door nail. I'll jist tie him behind the saddle and take him to the ranch and skin him.'
>
> After I got him tied on good, I climbed on ole Roan and headed for the ranch, jist goin' along thinkin' what a damn fine wolf I had. Then, sudden as hell, that ole wolf come to life and grabbed ole Roan in the flank, and boys, that damned ole gentle horse throwed me, saddle, wolf, and all, right out there in the middle of the flat and went skedaddlin' toward the ranch. Jist left me settin' there on my saddle.

Well, boys, I tell you I cussed that damned ole horse for ever'-thing I knowed of. I jist had to cuss that time.

His conversion took so well that Ole Mass became something of a lay preacher. Sometimes when he was in a cowtown on business, preacher friends invited him to give the sermon. With his inborn rhetoric and acting skill, he could put a congregation into tears.

Aged and infirm, Ole Mass and Ole Miss moved to Valentine. Henry Mayfield's love for his friends stands out in one of the few letters he ever wrote, this to the sons of ranch couple Zack and Exa Means. He wrote:

Sam & Joe   Hulie & Dub   Lee and Paul
My Dear Boys Dont forget to Bow your heds at .9.o.clock Ever Knight and Plead and Pray With Our Father in heven to Save your Mother and She Will recover and Come to helth and Bea With us all a gaine.
God Bless you all I Can not rite any more My Eyes is So ful of Tears.
God Bless you all
H Mayfield.

In 1935 Ole Mass died at age ninety-one. Will and Joe Evans, sons of his hunting partner George Evans, wrote about him in their books, *Border Skylines* and *The Cowboys' Old Hitchin' Post*.

The Big Owner will never forget you,
He knows every action and look;
So for safety you'd better get branded,
Have your name in that great Talley Book.
—"A Cowboy's Dream"

Notes on Sources

1.

Terlingua Desert Tales

Anne Sonora Ellis wrote of her experience with the Adobe Walls mystery bells in a 1968 Sul Ross State University student paper, "Echoes of the Past: Folktales of the Big Bend Country," which also includes the story of Jesusita. An account of the shoot-out at Adobe Walls is found in Hallie Stillwell, *How Come It's Called That: Place Names in the Big Bend Country* (New York: October House, 1968), pp. 12–13. The trouble caused by Bass Outlaw at Fronteriza is described in Jack Martin, *Border Boss: Captain John R. Hughes—Texas Ranger* (San Antonio: Naylor Co., 1942), pp. 76–82.

As for the name of Terlingua, Frances Tovar of Alpine, who grew up there, said some of the oldsters referred to Terlingua Abaja as *Pantalones Mocho* (cut-off jeans). She did not know why.

Walter Fulcher's inquiry into the origin and meaning of the name is found in his *The Way I Heard It: Tales of the Big Bend*, ed. Elton Miles (Austin: University of Texas Press, 1959), p. 47. Further inquiry and comment by Fulcher seems to be contained in a lost Fulcher manuscript quoted by Pauline Cepeda in an SRSU student paper, "History of Terlingua," 1949. Cepeda's paper is in the Clifford B. Casey Collection, Archives of the Big Bend, Wildenthal Memorial Library, SRSU.

For allusion to John Glanton's massacre of Indians at Terlingua Abaja, see Elton Miles, *Tales of the Big Bend* (College Station: Texas A&M University Press, 1976), p. 121. Henry Fletcher's remarks are in "Placenames Are Significant . . ." in the 60th anniversary edition of the *Alpine Avalanche*, September 14, 1951, p. 40. Fletcher's article on the Trans-Pecos region first appeared in the *Avalanche* in 1941. For W. W.

Newcomb's placement of the Shawnees in Texas, see his *The Indians of Texas from Prehistoric to Modern Times* (Austin: University of Texas Press, 1969), p. 384. Dr. Robert T. Hill's "saddle blanket" theory was brought out in *Tales of Terlingua* (Jan.–Feb., 1981), p. 4, publication of the Merramar land development company for the Terlingua Ranch Property Owners Association.

Lieutenant Echols's report of "Lates Lengua" is found in a photocopy excerpt from U.S. Senate, *Index to Executive Documents*, 36th Cong., 9 vols. (Washington, D.C.: George W. Bowman, Printer, 1861), [II?], 47, 48. This copy is in the Wildenthal Memorial Library, SRSU. A. B. Johnson, *Johnson's Texas* (New York: Privately printed, 1886), includes a map bearing the name "Latislengua." My fair copy is the source of C. S. Broadbent's allusion to "Terlingua" and the "three languages" tradition: bibliographical details are lost. "Tasa Linga" is named in Brewster County Deed of Trust and Mortgage Record, vol. 5, p. 268. References to pamphlets by O. W. Williams, privately printed in Fort Stockton, Texas, are: *My Dear Children*, dated January 25, 1902; and *By the Campfire in the Southwest*, dated March 7, 1902. Dr. T. H. Campbell expressed his opinion about the joint origin of *tezuino* and Terlingua in a letter to me, dated December 26, 1990.

Late in 1976 Dolores Latorre of Austin, Texas, wrote, "Terlingua is derived from the Spanish word *terlinguaita*, meaning "quicksilver" (undated clipping, *Austin American-Statesman*, [December?], 1976). In her letter to me, January 10, 1977, Ms. Latorre said that she encountered the word in a Spanish encyclopedia, which she cited as *Union tipografica editorial Hispano Americano*, IX:1274. My attempts to locate an encyclopedia with this title were unsuccessful.

In fact, the naming process happened the other way around, as an oxychloride of mercury was first identified about 1903 at the Terlingua mines and therefore named terlinguaite — in Spanish, *terlinguaita*. Alpine geologist Dr. Frank W. Daughtery, in a letter of November 11, 1989, called my attention to its identification and description in A. J. Moses, "Egglestonite, Terlinguaite, and Montroydite, New Minerals from Terlingua, Texas," *American Journal of Science*, 4th ser., 14, (1903) 253–63.

Terlingua miners called quicksilver *azogue*, a universal Spanish term.

2.

The San Vicente Rain Dance

The principal source of information about the *matachina* in San Vicente and Midland is an unpublished Sul Ross State University student paper by Gilbert Sanchez, in possession of Miriam Lowrance of Alpine, a retired professor of art, SRSU. Mrs. Lowrance also provided photographs and an audio tape of a Midland *matachina* tune.

The fullest description of a San Vicente rain dance seems to be that of J. O. Langford in *Big Bend: A Homesteader's Story* (Austin: University of Texas Press, 1955), pp. 87–91, with photographic illustrations, p. 120. Langford imparted a few supplemental details to Ethel Nail, who wrote about them in "Are Rainmakers Fakes?" in AnneJo Wedin, *The Magnificent Marathon Basin: A History of Marathon, Texas, Its People and Events* (Austin: Nortex Press, 1989), pp. 548–49. Haldeen Braddy gives his account in *Mexico and the Old Southwest: People, Places, and Palaver* (Port Washington, N.Y.: Kennikat Press, 1971), pp. 173–75.

The Trinidad, New Mexico, *matachina* of 1881 is described in Honora DeBusk Smith, "Mexican Plazas along the River of Lost Souls" in *Southwestern Lore*, ed. J. Frank Dobie, Publications of the Texas Folklore Society No. 9 (Dallas: Southwest Press: 1931), pp. 72–75. The Yaqui *matachina* is described in *A Treasury of Mexican Folkways* (New York: Crown Publishers, 1947), pp. 336–37. Other New Mexican *matachinas* are described in Flavia Waters Champe, *The Matachines Dance of the Upper Rio Grande: History, Music, and Choreography* (Lincoln: University of Nebraska Press, 1965), especially pp. 1, 51, 82–96.

Informative and useful is Gertrude Prokosch Kurath, "Mexican Moriscas: A Problem in Dance Acculturation," *Journal of American Folklore* (April–June, 1949): 87–106. Gertrude P. Kurath in "The Origin of the Pueblo Indian Matachines," *El Palacio* (September–October, 1957): 259–64, tries to establish an Arabic origin for the word *matachina*.)

3.
The Orient Railroad

As in each chapter of this book, tale tellers and other informants are usually named along with their stories and information. An important source of tales is Victor J. Smith, "Tales of the Kansas City, Mexico, and Orient Railroad," *Mesquite and Willow*, Publications of the Texas Folklore Society No. 27 (Dallas: Southern Methodist University Press, 1952), pp. 162–70.

Details concerning construction and financing come from John L. Kerr and Frank Donovan, *Destination Topolobampo: The Kansas City, Mexico, and Orient Railroad* (San Marino, Calif.: Golden West Books, 1968); and Clarence O. Senior, "The Kansas City, Mexico, and Orient

Railroad," M.A. thesis, University of Missouri, n.d. Supplementary matter is contained in Arthur E. Stilwell, *Cannibals of Finance* (Chicago: Farnum Publishing Co., 1912).

After completing this work, I became aware of a regular column by Jack R. Davenport, "Dead-Heading along the Orient," which appeared in the *San Angelo Daily Standard* around July 26, 1925, p. 2.

4.
Progress, Revolution, and Recovery

The Orient's involvement with West Texas oil towns is reported by N. Ethie Eagleton in *On the Last Frontier: A History of Upton County, Texas* (El Paso: Texas Western Press, 1971), pp. 18, 20, 80. Memories of trade in Alpine water are found in Sam T. Mallison, *The Great Wildcatter* (Charleston: Education Foundation of West Virginia, 1953), p. 345.

Useful Big Bend history of the Orient Railroad is contained in Clifford B. Casey, *Mirages, Mystery, and Reality: Brewster County, Texas, the Big Bend of the Rio Grande* (Seagraves, Texas: Pioneer Book Publications, 1976), pp. 194–99; and Alice Virginia Cain, "A History of Brewster County," M.A. thesis, SRSU, 1939, pp. 96–104. As in chapter 3, use is made of Kerr and Donovan, *Destination Topolobampo.*

Arthur E. Stilwell's only visit to Alpine and his last visit to San Angelo are reported in the *Alpine Avalanche*, Feb. 20, 1913, p. 3.

5.
Boom, Bust, and Survival

Once more, useful sources are Kerr and Donovan, *Destination Topolobampo*, and Eagleton, *On the Last Frontier.*

Stories about building the railroad from Chihuahua to Ojinaga are from Antonio Delgado, "El Kansas City, México, y Oriente — Memorias de Marco Tono," *Chihuahua Opinion*, July 13, 1984, p. 4. Those which tell about the line between Creel and Topolobampo are from the article by Don Burgess, "Mexican Railway . . ." *Alpine Avalanche*, August 20, 1958, p. 1B.

A source is J. S. Allhands, "Reopening the Chihuahua Trail," *Voice of the Mexican Border* (Marfa, Texas), Centennial Edition, 1936, pp. 68–76. As in chapter 3, stories by V. J. Smith come from his "Tales of the Kansas City, Mexico, and Orient Railroad," *Mesquite and Willow.*

6.
Bandits in the Big Bend

J. O. Langford describes the bandit scare at Hot Springs in *Big Bend: A Homesteader's Story* (Austin: University of Texas Press, 1955), pp. 141–44, 148–51. Information about Jesse Deemer is found in Clifford B. Casey's *Mysteries, Mirages, and Reality*, pp. 113, 115, 131–33, 37. Robberies near Alpine and the posse's pursuit of bandits are reported in "Mexicans Raid Brewster County Ranches," "Mexicans Escaped," and "Need the Soldiers," *Alpine Avalanche*, February 20, 1913, pp. 2, 3; also "Sheriff Walton Given Authority to Act" and "Governor Colquitt Acts," *Alpine Avalanche*, February 27, 1913, pp. 2, 3. The latter story reports the possible sending of U.S. troops to Mexico and the governor's deployment of Texas State Guard units. The attempt to wreck a train near Alpine is mentioned in Ronnie C. Tyler, *The Big Bend* (Washington, D.C.: National Park Service, 1975), p. 165.

7.
The Glenn Springs Horror

The three points of view — those of Compton, the soldiers, and "Cap" Wood — are pieced together from several sources.

Objective historical sources are Casey, *Mysteries, Mirages, and Reality*, pp. 129–34; Carlisle Graham Raht, *Romance of the Davis Mountains and Big Bend Country* (El Paso: Rahtbooks, 1919), pp. 350–58; Ronnie C. Tyler, *The Big Bend: A History of the Last Texas Frontier* (Washington, D.C.: National Park Service, 1975), pp. 165–69.

O. G. Compton told of his and his children's ordeal in his testimony published in *Investigation of Mexican Affairs*, Senate Document 285, 66th Cong. (Series No. 7665–7666), (Washington, D.C.: Government Printing Office, 1920), pp. 1059–63.

One of two military points of view is that in letters and reports of Capt. C. W. Cole now lodged in the U.S. National Archives: RG-393: Records of the U.S. Army Continental Command, E-55 General Correspondence, Big Bend Military District, 1919–1920, 600.5 Camp at Glenn Springs. This correspondence contains copies of the 1916 reports by Capt. Cole supporting the unsuccessful effort to rename the post for Pvt. Hudson Rodgers, who was killed in the raid. The moving letter by Sgt. Smyth also is contained in this file.

James Hopper describes Sgt. Smyth in "A Little Mexican Punitive Expedition," *Collier's*, July 15, 1916, pp. 5–6, where he also reports rumors about Jesse Deemer. Another soldier's point of view is that of Lt. Col. William A. Raborg, Ret., "The Villa Raid on Glenn Springs," November 22, 1954, unpublished documented memoir, Archives of the Big Bend, Widenthal Memorial Library, SRSU.

C. D. Wood's brief first report of his view of the raid is included in his letter to Captain Cole, found in U.S. National Archives file RG-393, which he wrote a day or two after the raid. Wood later testified at length before the Senate committee investigating "Mexican Affairs," and he used that printed testimony almost verbatim in his "The Glenn Springs Raid," *Sul Ross State College Bulletin* 43:3, Publications of the West Texas Historical and Scientific Society No. 19, September 1, 1963, pp. 65–71.

Brief biographical data on the slain soldiers and the Compton boy are preserved in the death records of Brewster County, Texas.

Exaggerations and legends of various events are found in "Glenn Spring Raid," *Alpine Avalanche*, May 11, 1916, p. 2; Wally George, "Tequila and Gunpowder," *True West*, November–December, 1958, pp. 12–13, 34–37; and Frances Springfield, "The Glenn Springs Raid" in AnneJo Wedin, *The Magnificent Marathon Basin*.

8.
The Boquillas Robbery and Kidnapping

The fear in Alpine of bandit attack produced "Instructions for Members of the Home Guard," *Alpine Avalanche*, May 18, 1916, p. 1.

The Boquillas raid is briefly described in Captain Cole's report of May 13, 1916, in U.S. National Archives RG-393. Most of that report, including Sergeant Smyth's letter, is included in Raht, *Romance of the Davis Mountains and Big Bend Country*, pp. 350–57.

Information about Jesse Deemer is contained in Casey, *Mystery, Mirages, and Reality*. Both Deemer and Payne are characterized by Hopper in "A Little Mexican Punitive Expedition."

The most complete account of Payne's misfortune in the Boquillas raid is that of Marcello Payne in "The Monroe Payne Family" in Wedin, *The Magnificent Marathon Basin*, pp. 449–50.

Details of the robberies of Deemer and Alcala and of the alleged murders are filed in the Brewster County/District Clerk's criminal court records in Brewster County.

Accounts of the robbery of the Puerto Rico mine store and the abduction of mine personnel are found in Lieutenant Colonel Raborg's "The Villa Raid on Glenn Springs"; W. D. Smithers, *Pancho Villa's Last Hideout – On Both Sides of the Rio Grande in the Big Bend Country*

(Alpine: West Texas Scientific Society and Sul Ross State College n.d.; and George, "Tequilla and Gunpowder."

In 1932 Dr. Powers posted his sign in Big Lake, Texas, having been in the medical profession for fifty-five years, according to "Slaying of Barnett Described," *San Angelo Standard-Times*, March 24, 1932.

9.
The Cavalry Strikes Back

Principal sources are Hopper, "A Little Mexican Punitive Expedition;" Tyler, *The Big Bend*; and Raborg, "The Villa Raid on Glenn Springs. It is Raborg who outlines the expedition's route along several villas and *rancheritos* in Mexico. A more recent historical study of the action is Ronnie C. Tyler, "The Little Punitive Expedition in the Big Bend," *Southwestern Historical Quarterly* (January, 1975): 271–91.

Tales about Monroe Payne were picked up from oral tradition by Russell M. Drake, a free-lance writer from Lake Elsinore, California. Marcello Payne tells of his father's last days in "The Monroe Payne Family." Facts concerning Monroe Payne's death are confirmed in the death records of Brewster County.

10.
Bandits on Trial — Guardsmen on Guard and in Print

Natividad Alvarez was charged with the murder of the soldiers in Criminal Indictments 923, 924, and 925, which are on file with the Brewster County/District Clerk, Alpine, Texas. Though Indictment 922 against Alvarez is missing, there can be little doubt that it names him as the killer of the Compton boy. Trial records for that alleged murder are in the office of the Jeff Davis County/District clerk in Fort Davis, Texas. Indictment 911 charged Natividad with the armed robbery of Jesse Deemer, for which he was found guilty and sentenced to the penitentiary.

Juan Portillo was charged with armed robbery in Indictment 938, and Mariano Ayatola with looting Deemer's store of flour in Indictment 941. In Indictment 918 Marcario Alvarez was charged with armed robbery, for which he was tried and sentenced at Sanderson, Texas. See Terrell County/District Clerk trial record of *The State of Texas* vs. *Marcario Alvarez*.

The Jodie Harris material comes from the Jodie Harris Collection in the Archives of the Big Bend, SRSU. This collection includes his two newspapers, *La Noria*, October 25, 1916, and *The Big Bend*, November 30, 1916; many of his post cards; and a clipping from the *Fort Worth Star-Telegram* by Frank Friauf, "Soldier Serving in the Big Bend in 1916 Saw Area's National Park Potential." Also with the collection is a biographical sketch of Jodie Harris prepared by archives personnel.

Ronnie C. Tyler comments on the attitude of some guardsmen in "The Little Punitive Expedition," p. 291. For several of Harris's cartoons see Tyler's "Protecting the Big Bend — A Guardsman's View," *Southwestern Historical Quarterly* (January, 1975).

11.
The Big Bend Tablet

Before getting down to sources, the reader might be interested in a related "esoteric" item. Two years before anybody had any idea of what the inscription said, Bernice McGee received a letter dated June 26, 1972, from Mrs. Ezell Eiland of El Paso, who asserted that she was a master graphologist with twenty years of experience and was "recognized in the courts of Texas as a handwriting expert." In poring over the picture of the inscription (in the August issue of *True West*) with a magnifying glass, she concluded, "Due to the uneven pressure exerted on the writing instrument — the corrugations and other indications shown — your writer was very ill physically. It appears to have been written under stress. This is a writer who would love good food well seasoned. . . . He was self-reliant with a keen mentality. He was scientific minded and had engineering ability — the ability to build and work with his hands. . . . He would want to find out for himself — he wanted to explore and analyze what he had found. . . . He was not a young man and he wasn't a very old man."

In a telephone interview, August 25, 1990, Donald Uzzell told me the story of his finding the tablet fragments and his opinion as to their durability. Earlier, not knowing that Donald, because of a hereditary, degenerative condition, cannot write, I had "cross-examined" him in a letter. The reply came from his wife, Reva, dictated by Donald (her letter dated August 17, 1990). Donald's account as presented in this chapter combines information from that letter and the interview.

Bernice and Jack McGee told of joining the Uzzells and the Nickleses at Hot Springs to relocate the tablet's hiding place in "The Mystery of the Big Bend Tablet," *True West*, July–August, 1972, pp. 10–15, 42–47, 50. Here they also told how Donald made his discovery and concluded that the tablet must have been made of bentonite. In a letter to Miriam Lowrance, July 5, 1977, Bernice McGee reported that David Evan "left it lay in a window sill until it was destroyed."

Dr. Barry Fell's map of the distribution of ancient non-American epigraphs in the United States appears in *Saga America* (New York: Time Books, 1980), p. 230. The same book contains photographs of the Big Bend tablet and the Los Lunas Ten Commandments, pp. 164, 167.

Dr. Cyclone Covey's examination of Tornillo Creek bentonite is referred to in Bernice McGee's letter to Miriam Lowrance, January 15, 1971. Her exuberant report to Miriam about Dr. Fell's translation is in her letter of July 5, 1977. (A description by Dr. Fell of the Iberean alphabet occurs in his *Bronze Age America* [Boston: Little, Brown & Co., 1982], p. 34.)

The epigraphers' rating scale is taken from William R. McClone and Philip M. Leonard, *Ancient Celtic America* (Fresno, Calif.: Panorama West Books, 1986), Table II, pp. 42–43, and Table III, p. 44. This work gives an account of the Los Lunas inscription with evidence for and against its authenticity. Bernice McGee spoke of the double-bladed axe in a letter to me, September 15, 1990; Dr. Frank W. Daugherty's description of bentonite is contained in a letter to me, May 8, 1990; and the remarks by Dr. J. Charles Kelley are from my notes of our conversation, May 6, 1990.

12.
Cowboys and God

Some of the preachers in the Old West are named by Mody C. Boatright in *Folk Laughter in the American Frontier* (1944; reprint, New York: Collier Books, 1961), p. 139. Also, Boatright tells a variation of the linerider story. Otherwise, yarns spun here are in oral tradition.

Rev. L. R. Millican narrates his life story in his *Sermon and Very Short Life Sketch of L. R. Millican, Over Forty Years a Missionary in West Texas*, "Printed at the Request of a Great Many Friends" (El Paso, 1930?), pp. 1–13. He presents his exemplum of cattle breaking out of pen on p. 20. Other biographical details concerning Millican are based on Kathy Stokes, *Paisano: The Story of a Cowboy and a Camp Meeting* (Waco: Texian Press, 1980).

Will F. Evans recollects the genesis of the Bloys Camp Meeting in *Border Skylines: Fifty Years of "Tallying Out" on the Bloys Camp Meeting Ground*, published for the Bloys Camp Meeting Association by Cecil Baugh, Dallas, Texas, 1940. He gives his account of Rev. William B.

Bloys on pp. 157–63; of Rev. L. R. Millican, pp. 171–73; John Z. Means, pp. 192–97; George W. Evans, pp. 192–201; and Henry B. Mayfield, pp. 220–26. He recollects work and play, with accounts of camp cooks and the men's prayer tree, on pp. 297–371. On pp. 461–67 is the story of "Ole Mass" in the cow pen, with the hilarious tank baptizing on pp. 467–68.

Joe M. Evans remembers early times at Bloys in *A Corral Full of Stories* (El Paso: McMath Co., n.d.), pp. 18–23. In *The Cowboy's Hitchin' Post* (El Paso, [1947?]), Joe describes events at the Bloys "come clean" meetings. He tells also about events and prayer trees at camp meetings he helped to establish in the West.

Index